3/07

How to Repair Your Credit Report

A Step-by-Step Manual on How to Increase Your Credit Score...Guaranteed!

How to Repair Your Credit Report

A Step-by-Step Manual on How to Increase Your Credit Score...Guaranteed!

Emmanuel Ike, MBA

How to Repair Your Credit Report

NOTICE

This publication and the accompanying materials are designed to provide accurate and authoritative information in regard to the subject matter covered in it. It is sold with the understanding that the publisher is not engaged in rendering legal, accounting or other professional opinions. If legal advice or other expert assistance is required, the services of a competent professional should be sought. (From a Declaration of Principles adopted jointly by a Committee of the American Bar Association and a Committee of Publishers and Associations.)

Publisher's guarantee: We understand there are people who would like to take advantage of the system, and you're not one of them. Because of the proprietary nature of the materials in this book, if you want a refund because your credit score did not increase after using the guidelines in this book, we ask that you return the book in re-saleable condition to the publisher within thirty days with proofs and we will gladly refund your money. There are no refunds from retailers.

How to Repair Your Credit Report
ISBN 0-9770693-3-8
Library of Congress Number 2006903616
Printed in the United States of America.

 SOW Publishing

P.O. Box 702063, Dallas, TX 75370, USA. www.sowpublishing.com

10 9 8 7 6 5 4 3 2 1

ABOUT THE AUTHOR

Emmanuel Ike is an expert in accounting software, database management, and spreadsheet programming. He has been an accountant for more than 12 years, specializing in cash flow, asset management, and financial reporting. He teaches individuals and small businesses about credit and credit reporting and as a hobby, he enjoys aggressive legal research. Mr. Ike has a Bachelor of Science degree in accounting and a Master's degree in finance with honors. He also has a certificate in private investigation and holds a diploma in the legal assistant program, specializing in legal and medical research from a prestigious law school. Mr. Ike is an author, publisher, and entrepreneur.

ACKNOWLEDGMENTS

I wish to extend a special thank you and my profound appreciation to all the customers who bought my first credit score book. You advised me to write a how—to manual that has less to do with reading and much more to do with doing. I have heard your concerns about information overload, and have responded with a step-by-step manual, easy-to-use manual—that will help to increase your credit score. I dedicate this book to you, my customers, who found out how easy it is to increase your credit score by using my book.

NOTICE

Dedication

This book is dedicated to my family, especially my father who taught me that wisdom, understanding, power, and concentration are the keys to success. And to my mother who taught me that love—beauty, kindness, peace, and integrity—is the key to life.

Contents

How to Repair Your Credit Report

Introduction

You know as well as I do that interest rates are your number one financial enemy, and the key to defeating your enemy is increasing your credit score. Who says you have to pay 10, 15 or even 20% interest rates while others are paying zero percent? Who says you have to work all day only to hand over your hard-earned money to someone else in the name of high interest rate? What are you going to do about it? Nothing?

Don't just sit there and continue to take it, day after day. Enough is enough—get up and do something! It's time you pulled the plug on high interest rates—and the time is now! Originally, banks charged interest rates on people who borrowed money from them, and credit scores were used only to find out if those borrowers would be able to give the banks back their money.

Not anymore! It's gotten complicated!
Did you say, "It's none of my business, I don't borrow money."
That's what you think! Everything you do now depends on your credit score. If you can't beat them join them is the name of the game!

The following entities are looking into your credit report right now: *employers, insurance companies, mortgage lenders, auto finance companies, landlords, credit card companies, department stores, furniture stores, utility companies, school loan lenders, collection agencies, judgment creditors, government agencies, banks, savings and loans, credit unions, and a host of other businesses with "legitimate business needs."* The list is endless! Yep, you got it! Every business is judging you by your credit score. And a low credit score is robbing you. It's time to fight back!

I know you're asking yourself, "Who created this credit score?" YOU! Yes, you did! You have been creating a low credit score for yourself without knowing it all these years. You can start creating a good credit score today, and I can show you how. You've heard it before, "No credit, no problem! Bad credit, no problem!" What they don't tell you is, "We are taking you to the cleaners!

So you've been living with a low credit score and a high interest rate?
So businesses have been taking advantage of your credit score ignorance?
"How did you know that?" you ask.

You just told me!
You just told me you've not been getting all your applications approved.
You just told me you've not been checking your credit report every year.
You just told me you've not been getting zero percent interest on a car loan.
And you just told me you've been walking around with a hole in your pocket, losing more than $4,000 a year—think about it!

I got it! "I'll just pay a credit repair company," you say. No! No! No! Bad idea! It's like paying your friend to attend Alcoholics Anonymous for you. That's cheating no one but yourself! This is something you do yourself. You go through the painful cleaning process yourself to learn what drinking is doing to you, to learn how to stay sober, to learn how to avoid relapse—all by yourself. It's not just about drinking; it's about your life. The same with credit repair, when you go through this system, you will learn how a low score is causing you to pay more in interest, to have low cash flow, to make late payments, to have low credit score—the cycle starts again. This is the perpetual cycle of negative cash flow. It's not just about making more money; it's about keeping it. It's not just about fixing your credit report; it's about keeping a high credit score—forever! About 110% of the people who repaired their own credit have gone on to become financially successful because they finally learned what was stealing their money—a high interest rate. When you repair your own credit report, everybody wins, because you buy more and pay more, this time, with wisdom! "I'll do it tomorrow," you say. What if you can't find this book tomorrow? There is only today! Think about it!

The only way you can get a high credit score is by planning! Plan the following:

Check your credit report at least once a year.
Repair your credit by dealing with credit bureaus.

Repair your credit by dealing with merchants, if any. Repair your credit by dealing with collection agencies, if any.
Make sure no one checks your credit report without your knowledge.
Use aggressive strategies to repair and enhance your credit score.

When you buy a car or house with a low credit score you are paying for the price of the car or house many times over. It doesn't have to be like that. It's no one's fault, but yours! What you don't know can kill you—but not any more. I have good news for you! You have in your hands a book that will show you the way—to a high credit score. This is the most powerful step-by-step book on repairing and improving your credit report ever; everything is laid out for you, all the forms and all the letters you would ever need, are included. What is it worth? It's priceless!

This book is divided into chapters. Chapters one through three will give you simple steps and checklists on how to repair your credit report. Chapters four through six are very practical. This is the heartbeat of the system; it's all about taking action! These are lists on what to do and when to do them—with speed and accuracy. The system is very powerful and the results will astound you—all in an easy-to-read user-friendly format. I will walk you through a sample credit report—showing you step by step how to repair your own credit report from beginning to end. Chapters seven through 10 will teach you strategies on demanding and negotiating boldly with credit bureaus, merchants, and collection agencies to get them to comply with your demands—with the law on your side. If you want your heart to start pumping, browse through chapter twelve on how to add new entries to your credit report—the information will amaze you! With the tool in your hands, the road to a higher credit score is clear and the ride is easy. Are you ready? When you start receiving your credit reports and your credit scores start going up, and at the end you say, "Wow, what a book," I have succeeded!

Congratulations! You have taken the first step on your road to a higher credit score. If you follow the steps I've outlined in this book, your credit score will NEVER be the same—guaranteed!

Chapter 1

Steps to Increasing Your Credit Score

Steps to Increasing Your Credit Score

U nderstanding the steps to increasing your credit score is very important. Once you understand the road map to your destination, the job is half done, and your success is assured. I have simplified the process and have broken it down into a scientific system where the outcome is predictable. Namely, there are only two steps. Yes, that's it! Only two major steps to improving your credit report: Cleaning your report and adding new entries to your report. Throughout this book, I'll continue to repeat these two central themes enough so that you can repeat it to yourself any time you hear about credit scores. Cleaning and adding are the two key words you should remember every time you think of credit scores.

Cleaning Your Credit Report

Cleaning your credit score involves seven easy strategies, which I have explained thoroughly in this book. These strategies are very practical and have been outlined for you—for easy learning and comprehension, and they include the following:

Seven strategies to cleaning your credit report:

- ❖ Request your credit report
- ❖ Spread your credit report
- ❖ Set up your credit score binder
- ❖ Work with credit bureaus
- ❖ Work with merchants
- ❖ Work with collection agencies
- ❖ Work with government agencies

Adding Entries to Your Credit Report

Both steps—cleaning and adding entries—are essential to increasing your credit score. However, adding entries to your credit report is much more important. By adding new entries, you are enhancing the status and power of your credit report with name brand merchants, enough to neutralize the effects of any negative entries. Also, with time, negative entries will drop off from your credit report, but new positive entries will stay for a long time on your report—for prospective merchants to see.

If you have 10 or more negative entries or more on your credit report, the best place to start right away is adding entries to your credit report. This statement is very important but only a few people know about it. If you have 10 negative entries or more, the first step to increasing your credit score is to go to a credit union or a bank and get a secured personal loan of $500 or more for nine months; and the second step is to find any negative entries on your credit report of $100 or less and pay them off immediately. Do not attempt these strategies until you have read the chapters on these topics. Adding entries to your credit report has eight easy strategies and they include the following:

Eight strategies to adding new entries to your credit report:

- ❖ By opening a credit card account
- ❖ By opening a jewelry store account
- ❖ By opening a furniture store account
- ❖ By opening a department store account
- ❖ By opening an appliance store account
- ❖ By opening an electronic store account
- ❖ By using your relative's or friend's account
- ❖ By using a credit union personal loan

Chapter 2

Checklist for Increasing Your Credit Score

Checklist for Increasing Your Credit Score

The purpose of this section is to summarize all the activities you would be using to increase your credit score. I want to make it easy so you don't have to wonder about what to do next. This is a general guideline; you do not need to use all the items on the checklist to receive the highest credit score. I'm being thorough to make sure you have every possible scenario at your finger tips. Individual credit situations will vary and this will make you skip some steps. Please note all sample letters that are referred to in this list are included in this book. The following items are included in the checklist:

1. Decide if you want a free credit report or a paid credit report with score from the credit bureaus. A free report does not have a credit score, but a paid credit report has a credit score you can see right away.

2. If you want the free annual credit report, visit www.annualcreditreport.com or write the Annual Credit Report Request Service, P.O. Box 105283, Atlanta, GA 30348-5283. The law allows you a free annual credit report from the three credit bureaus, every 12 calendar months—no questions asked!

3. If you want a paid credit report with score directly from the individual credit bureaus, visit www.equifax.com, www.experian.com, and www.transunion.com to research addresses and prices of credit reports with scores.

4. If you want a three-in-one paid credit report with score from VantageScore, a company owned by three credit bureaus, visit www.vantagescore.com for the price of a credit report with score.

5. Spread your credit report using the steps listed in this book.

6. Buy a three-ring binder with 10 tabs, set up your binder, and file your credit reports.

7. Complete the list of negatives and the list of positives sections for your binder.

8.   Write letters to the credit bureaus to correct personal information and delete outdated entries from your credit reports, if necessary.

9.   Write letters to the merchants to correct information, delete entries or provide proof of information, if necessary.

10. Write letters to the collection agencies to correct information, delete entries or provide proof of information, if necessary.

11. Write letters to companies to delete inquiries they made on your credit report without your consent, if any, or provide proof of information. You must request and receive their names and addresses the first time you request your credit report from the credit bureaus.

12. Write the Federal Trade Commission, your state Attorney General, and the Better Business Bureau if anyone is giving you a hard time. This may not be necessary.

13. If you receive proof of information from merchants and collection agencies, confirm by checking documentation that the account is actually yours.

14. If you cannot wait for the entry to expire on its own, strategically negotiate a payment method—one-time, full payment with a big discount, monthly scheduled payments, or partial payment with monthly scheduled payments.

15. Before you send payments, you must send letters of agreement to merchants and collection agencies, and receive back the signed agreement from them.

16. Request an updated copy of your credit report to verify that credit bureaus, merchants, and collection agencies have deleted negative entries as promised; also review credit report for reinsertion.

17.   Write letters to the merchants to confirm account histories and send copies of the letters to credit bureaus to add new entries to your credit report.

18.   Open a credit card account (apply for a minimum line of credit) and a credit union personal loan, make all payments on time and pay off the personal loans in nine to 12 months. See details in the book

19.   Open a furniture loan (apply for a minimum line of credit), make all payments on time and pay off furniture loan in nine months.

20.   Open a department store credit card (apply for a minimum line of credit) and jewelry store credit (apply for a minimum line of credit), and make all payments on time. Repeat the credit union personal loan, furniture loan, and jewelry loan to add new entries to your credit report. Use other types of credit as detailed in this book to add new entries to your credit report.

21.   Every year request your free annual credit report, review and correct any mistakes. Monitor and maintain your high credit score.

22.   Congratulations! You are now in control of your credit life. Be wise, your tremendous high credit score will trigger an avalanche of junk mails from marketing companies trying to sell you something. Send letters to the three major credit bureaus and opt out of marketing and promotional databases.

Chapter 3

Request Your Credit Report

Research Addresses and Prices

Researching for addresses is extremely important not only for the credit bureaus, but also for the merchants and collection agents, because your communications—including letters and telephone calls—are time sensitive. You want all your letters delivered or returned to you only when the intended recipient is no longer at that address, not because you used the wrong address. The process of looking up addresses and prices is very easy if you apply the right methods as explained in this book. You want to make sure you're using the right information at all times when communicating with credit bureaus, merchants, and collection agencies to reduce mailing expenses that result from using incorrect addresses or credit report prices. Your task is to research for credit bureaus addresses and prices for a paid credit report. Write them down or print them from a computer if possible and file them in your credit binder.

If there is only one place you can go and find the current addresses to the three credit bureaus—it's the Internet! You don't know the importance of it until you receive a lot of return-to-sender mail. My goal is to show you all the land mines in the credit repairing process.

The Internet is the best place to find the addresses to the three major credit bureaus. However, I do not endorse buying a credit report through the Internet. On the Internet, you will only be researching for three things: the price of credit report with score, the address, and the phone number of the credit bureau. Be careful when copying addresses; sometimes credit bureaus pick repetitive post office box numbers and zip codes, such as 4555 or 4445, just to confuse the public. Note that the information on the Internet can and does change from time to time.

To find Equifax's address and the price of a credit report:

- Visit www.equifax.com.
- Click on **3-in-1 Credit Report**.
- Find the price of the 3-in-1 Credit Report with Score Power, and click the **Back** button at the top left of your monitor, to go to the previous page

- Click **Contact Us** at the top right of the home page (you may have to scroll up or look at the entire page).
- Find the mailing address to Equifax. This is where you will mail your check or money order for your credit report with score. You may see the following address:

Equifax Credit Information
P.O. Box 740241
Atlanta, GA 30374

- Find the telephone number for ordering your credit report over the phone. You may see the following telephone number:

1-800-685-1111

To find Experian's address and the price of a credit report:

- Visit www.experian.com.
- Click **Learn more** located under the Experian Credit Score (not 3 Bureaus Online Credit Report and not Experian Credit Report).
- Find the price of an Experian Credit Score, and click the **Back** button on the tool bar at the top left of your monitor (you may have to scroll up), to go to the previous page.
- Click **Contact Us** at the top right of the home page or look at the entire page.
- You may find the ordering phone number is: 1-888-397-3742 or 1-888-EXPERIAN (do not copy the corporate address or business address).
- Call 1-888-EXPERIAN and listen carefully for the address, probably a box number where you can mail your check or money order.
- Write the address as you listen. This is where you will mail your check or money order for your credit report with score. You may hear the following address:

Experian
P.O. Box 2104
Allen, TX 75013

To find TransUnion's address and the price of a credit report:

- Visit www.transunion.com.
- Find the price of Single Credit Report and Credit Score & Analysis (not Debt analysis unless you really need it). Click the **Back** button at the top left of your monitor to go to the previous page.
- Click **Contact Us** at the top right of the home page (you may have to scroll up or you may have to look at the entire page).
- Find the mailing address to TransUnion. This is where you will mail your check or money order for your credit report with score. You may see the following address:

TransUnion
P.O. Box 2000
Chester, PA 19022

- Find the telephone number for ordering your credit report over the phone. You may see the following telephone number:

1-800-888-4213

Request a Free Credit Report

There are two qualifications to getting your free credit report:

1. Adverse condition
2. Government mandate

Adverse condition. You would receive a free credit report from the credit bureaus if any of the following happened to you in the last 60 days:

- You have been denied credit.
- You have been denied employment.
- You have been denied insurance.
- You have been denied rental.

- You are unemployed.
- You are the recipient of public welfare.
- You are a victim of fraud.

I have heard instances where people initiate the denial of credit by using the following guidelines:

1. Find a merchant who reports to all three major credit bureaus.
2. Make sure the credit limit you are applying for is too high and you will get a denial letter.
3. After you receive your denial letter, write to all three major credit bureaus and enclose a copy of the denial letter.
4. Your letter must be indented to the left and include your name, address, and date, to make room for stapling your certified mail slip from the post office, if any.
5. You must write to the credit bureau for a free credit report.
6. You must request a list of names, addresses, and phone numbers of all subscribers—including merchants and collection agencies.
7. You must request complete and accurate account numbers of all accounts on your credit report.
8. You must request a list of names, addresses, and phone numbers of all inquiries.
9. You must request copies of dispute forms.
10. You must request consumer rights, both state and federal.

Government mandate. Why would you want to go through all that when the government has come to your rescue? Congress has passed a law that says you are entitled to receive an annual credit report free—no questions asked! Through the Fair and Accurate Credit Transactions Act (FACT Act), consumers are now allowed a free copy of their credit report every 12 months. To respond to this demand from the government, the three credit bureaus came together to create a company that would meet your requests. The name of the company is Annual Credit Report Request Services.

To find Annual Credit Report Service's address and phone number:

- Visit www.annualcreditreport.com.

- Click **Contact Us** at the top of the home page.
- Print or copy the address for mailing your correspondence to Annual Credit Report Services. You may find their address is:

Annual Credit Report Request Service
P.O. Box 105283
Atlanta, GA 30348-5283

- Copy the telephone number for ordering your credit report over the phone. You may find their phone number is (you may have to scroll down):

1-877-322-8228

Advantages of a Free Credit Report

- It is free and can be forwarded to you upon request after a credit denial.
- It is the best way to get your foot in the door of the credit bureau office.
- You may be assigned a credit report number, which you can use anytime to call or write the credit bureau.
- You would receive the current address and phone number of the credit bureau you are dealing with.
- You may not need a proof of identity because your letter of denial is your proof of identity.

Disadvantages of a Free Credit Report

A free credit report is a good place to start, but I do not recommend it because of the following disadvantages:

- Information on a free credit report may not be as reliable as information on the paid credit report.
- You will not receive your credit score, which is what you are trying to increase. It's very important to see your score to know where you currently stand.

Writing Your Letter

Most likely, this is your first time writing the credit bureaus, and the tone of your first letter would determine the way the credit bureaus would handle your reply and future communications. You must request the vital information you would need to accurately and completely correct your credit report. Send a follow-up letter if you do not get all the information you ask for. For example, names, addresses, and phone numbers of all merchants and collection agencies must be included in the reply package from the credit bureau. If you can find the information you are requesting from any one of the three credit reports, you're fine. Hence, you must wait for all three credit bureaus to reply before sending your follow-up letter. You may use the following steps to request your free credit report:

- Address your letter to the credit bureau's customer service manager.
- You need a free copy of your credit report because you were denied credit.
- You need a list of all subscribers, including merchants and collection agencies with addresses and phone numbers.
- You need complete and accurate account numbers of all accounts on your credit report.
- You need a list of names, addresses, and phone numbers of all inquiries on your credit report.
- You need copies of dispute forms.
- You need copies of state and federal consumer rights.
- You have enclosed copies of your Social Security card and utility bill for proof of identity.
- Be sure to send your letter to the credit bureaus within 60 days of receiving the denial letter.
- Send your letter by certified mail only without return receipt requested.

The following are two sample letters:

1. The first one is a free annual credit report you will request from Annual Credit Report Request Service. This is allowed by law once every 12 consecutive months, not just from January through December.

2. The second is a free credit report you will request from the individual credit bureaus because you were denied credit.

Therefore, you can request one free annual credit report and unlimited credit reports every time you are denied credit.

While you're using the sample letters in this book, be sure to see if there are small changes you need to make to suit your individual situation.

Sample Letter for a Free Credit Report

John Doe
1234 Adam St.
Dallas, TX 75111

January 1, 2004

Manager Customer Relations
Annual Credit Report Request Service
P.O. Box 105281
Atlanta, GA 30348-5281

Dear Manager:

I am requesting a copy of my annual free credit disclosure report. Please include the following in the package:

1.   Names, addresses, and phone numbers of all subscribers, including merchants and collection agencies
2.   Complete and accurate account numbers of all accounts on the report
3.   Names, addresses, and phone numbers of inquiries
4.   Copies of dispute forms
5.   Copies of state and federal consumer rights

My date of birth is January 1, 1900. Copies of Social Security card and utility bill are enclosed for proof of identity.

Your earliest reply is greatly appreciated.

Sincerely,

John Doe

Sample Letter for a Free Credit Report
(You're denied credit)

John Doe
1234 Adam St.
Dallas, TX 75111

January 1, 2004

Manager Customer Services
Equifax
P.O. Box 740241
Atlanta, GA 30374

Dear Manager:

ABC Company has denied me credit because of the information contained in my credit report. A copy of the denial letter is enclosed. I would like to have a free copy of my credit report, including the following information:

1. Names, addresses, and phone numbers of all subscribers, including merchants and collection agencies
2. Complete and accurate account numbers of all accounts on the report
3. Names, addresses, and phone numbers of inquiries
4. Copies of dispute forms
5. Copies of state and federal consumer rights

My date of birth is January 1, 1900. Copies of Social Security card and utility bill are enclosed for proof of identity.

Your earliest reply is greatly appreciated.

Sincerely,

John Doe

Request a Paid Credit Report

While I strongly favor the paid credit report with score, I DO NOT endorse buying them from the Internet. There are two ways of buying your credit report with score:

1.   Directly by mail from the three credit bureaus—Equifax, Experian, and TransUnion
2.   From VantageScore Solutions, LLC, a company created by the three credit bureaus

Directly from the credit bureaus. Most likely you have researched the credit bureaus addresses and the credit reports prices from the Internet. Now, you are going to write the individual credit bureaus, enclosing money orders for the price of the credit reports.

From VantageScore Solutions. You can get a paid credit report with score from just one source instead of going through the individual credit bureaus. The only advantage is that you will be able to compare your three scores side by side at one time, and be able to find out what entries are missing from any of the credit bureaus.

To find VantageScore Solutions' address and phone number:

- Visit www.vantagescore.com.
- Click **Contact Us** at the top of the home page.
- Copy the address of VantageScore. While writing this book, that information was not available.

Writing Your Letter

Your letter can be hand-written or typed, as long as it looks reasonably good. Your letter for a paid credit report should include the following information:

1.   Your letter should be indented to the left, including your name, address, and date.

2.   You must request and specify paid credit report with credit score.
3.   You must enclose the required amount for a paid credit report.
4.   You must request the list of names, addresses, and phone numbers of all subscribers—including merchants and collection agencies.
5.   You must request the complete and accurate account numbers of all accounts on your report.
6.   You must request a list of names, addresses, and phone numbers of all inquiries.
7.   You must request copies of dispute forms.
8.   You must request the consumer rights—both state and federal.
9.   You must include your Social Security number, your date of birth and a copy of your utility bill for proof of identity.
10.   Send your letter by certified mail without return receipt requested unless you want to, and type the certified receipt number on your letter.

It does not matter in what order you place this information, as long as the necessary information is contained in the letter. I recommend sending a money order, because personal checks might have to be cleared with your bank first and you don't want the credit bureaus to give your bank account information to their customers. You should send your letter by certified mail only without return receipt requested.

Tracking Your Mail

There are several ways to check whether your certified mail has reached its destination, but the easiest way is to follow these steps:

- Visit www.usps.com.
- Click **Track & Confirm** at the top of the home page.
- Type the certified mail number in the **Enter Label Number** text box; give space between the numbers to help you check the numbers you typed are correct. There are 20 numbers—five groups of four numbers.
- Click **Go**. You are taken to the shipping summary information window.
- Click **Print** at the top of your monitor to print the shipping details.
- Click **Shipment Details**.
- Click **Print** at the top of your monitor to print the shipping details.

Sample Letter for a Paid Credit Report

John Doe
1234 Adam St.
Dallas, TX 75111

January 1, 2004

Manager Customer Services
Equifax
P.O. Box 740241
Atlanta, GA 30374
Certified Mail #1234 5678 9123 4567 8912

Dear Manager:

I am enclosing the sum of $14.05 for my credit report with score. I would like to have the following information in your reply:

1. Names, addresses, and phone numbers of all subscribers, including merchants and collection agencies
2. Complete and accurate account numbers of all accounts on the report.
3. Names, addresses, and phone numbers of inquiries
4. Copies of dispute forms
5. Copies of state and federal consumer rights

My date of birth is January 1, 1900. Copies of Social Security card and utility bill are enclosed for proof of identity.

Your earliest reply is greatly appreciated.

Sincerely,

John Doe

What Reply to Expect from Credit Bureaus

After you have mailed your request for paid credit report with score, any one of the following could happen:

- Return to sender
- The credit bureau did not reply.
- The credit bureau wants more information.
- The credit bureau replied and included all the items requested.
- The credit bureau replied and included some or none of the items.

1.   Return to sender. Yes, sometimes you may receive a return-to-sender letter from the credit bureau. Because the credit bureau must reply to your letter within 15 days, the only reason your letter is returned to you is a wrong address. Use another address and re-send your letter.

2.   The credit bureau did not reply. The credit bureau will always reply and send your credit report if you had the correct address and enclosed the right fees for the report. If you did not have the right address, the letter would be returned to you. If after 30 days you did not receive your credit report, write a follow-up letter to the vice president of customer services and enclose a copy of your previous letter and a copy of your check or money order.

3.   The credit bureau wants more information. Any time you receive this kind of letter from the credit bureau after you send in the basic identification, it is a sign there is conflicting information. For example, you may be sharing the same name with another consumer, and be sure to check your credit report for accounts that do not belong to you. This might be a sign you're being mixed up with another person.

4.   The credit bureau replied and included all the items you requested. You should then start the review process. Make sure you have all the names, addresses, and phone numbers of all the merchants, collection agencies, and credit inquiries.

5.   The credit bureau replied and included some or none of the items you requested. Always remember the credit bureau has a policy of "don't ask, don't tell" so you must demand the information you need to verify your credit report. In this case, you would have to write a follow-up letter immediately and include the following requests and facts:

   a. Address it to the vice president of customer services
   b. Include the credit report number if you have any on your report
   c. Acknowledge the fact that you have received your credit report
   d. List only the items that were not included with your report
   e. State the fact that without these items, correcting your report is impossible
   f. Send by certified mail without return receipt requested and type the certified mail number on your letter.

It is important to remember to send all initial letters to the credit bureaus by certified mail only, and if you have access to the Internet, print the shipping detail for proof of delivery. Credit bureaus will reply to all your letters if you have the correct address within 15-30 days from the date of postage.

Sample Follow-up Letter for a Paid Credit Report

John Doe
1234 Adam St.
Dallas, TX 75111

January 1, 2004

Vice President Customer Services
Equifax
P.O. Box 740241
Atlanta, GA 30374
Certified Mail #1234 5678 9123 4567 8912

Dear Vice President:

I have just received my credit report bearing the number 999125125475. Your reply did not contain the following important credit information:

1. Complete and accurate account numbers of all accounts on the report.
2. Names, addresses, and phone numbers of inquiries.
3. Copies of state and federal consumer rights.

I would like these items to be mailed to me immediately. Without them, correcting my credit report is impossible.

Your immediate reply is greatly appreciated.

Sincerely,

John Doe

Chapter 4

Steps to Spreading Your Credit Report

Steps to Spreading Your Credit Report

Spreading your credit report is one of the most important and most rewarding tasks in repairing your credit—if done correctly. In spreading your report, you are meticulously analyzing every detail in the report with tools provided in this book. You are probing deeply, asking why, looking at blank spaces on your reports, and prying for hidden agendas. This is not reviewing a credit report which some credit repair companies and credit repair software companies do. Custom-made clothes cost more because of many reasons; one of them is quality. So is spreading your credit report. Before you start spreading your credit report, you must make a photocopy; if you mistakenly cross out a word or number, you want to be able to go back to the original. Now, let's go through the steps to spreading your credit report.

Your credit report would arrive in the mail in approximately 15-30 days from the time you sent your request—either the free or paid credit report. You should make a note of the date you received any credit report-related letter by writing, for example, "Recd 6/10/00" at the top of the credit letter or report.

Checking documentation. Spreading your credit reports starts with checking the contents of the mail package to make sure it has the following information:

- Your free or paid credit report with score
- List of merchants and subscribers including collection agencies with addresses and phone numbers. Sometimes, this is listed separately at the bottom of the main report after the inquiry section or as a part of each account entry line.
- Complete and correct account numbers of all accounts on your report, as a part of each entry line
- List of names, addresses, and phone numbers of all inquiries
- Dispute form, enclosed separately with your credit report
- Consumer rights—both state and federal—enclosed separately with your credit report

If you do not have any of these items, you must write the credit bureau immediately. Do not forget to include the report number, which is located at the top of the first page, if available. You are writing the credit bureau to send you the missing information. You should never accept any information over the phone from the credit bureau because you need proof for future reference. The names of merchants and other subscribers, including collection agencies, are of utmost importance to you and must be identified in the report. Let's look at the steps to spreading your credit report:

1. Proofreading Personal Information

In proofreading, you assume every entry in the personal identification information is wrong. All information is GUILTY until proven innocent! If your vital personal identification information is wrong, some information on your credit report is wrong too. With a red pen, you will check your name, current and previous addresses, Social Security number, date of birth, and current and previous places of employment. The only Social Security number that should be on your credit report is—yours, not your spouse's, your parents', or your children's. If the Social Security number is wrong, the entire credit report is wrong. There should be nothing like "formally known as" or "aliases" unless it is true, because ADDITIONAL names are used to insert false entries into your credit report. Look at the spelling of each word and the numbers very carefully, make sure they are yours, circle any information that is incorrect, and write "Delete or Correct" on the entry.

2. Tagging Positives

Tagging positive entries is done by putting a big check mark (✔) on all positive entries. When you open your credit report, you will look for the status name — and you will see words like "status," "current status," and "pay status." On the Equifax report, it is the last line or row on each entry, but on TransUnion and Experian reports it is in the last column on each entry. With a colored pen, you will first look for all positive status names, underline them, and put a big ✔ on the left margin of each entry. You will look for and underline the following positive status names:

- Paying as agreed
- Pays as agreed
- Paid satisfactorily

- Current
- Current, no late payments
- Paid/Never late
- Paid
- Paid closed
- Paid closed by customer

3. Tagging Negatives

After you finish tagging the positive, you will tag all the remaining entries with negatives. You tag negative entries by putting a big (**X**) mark on them. Double check when you're finished to make sure entries with a big **X** have negative remarks by the status names.

With a colored pen, you will first underline the status name and then put a big **X** on the left margin of the entry. You will look for and underline the following negative status names:

1. Current – 30, 60, 90, 120+ days late
2. Late payment
3. Delinquent
4. Charge-off
5. Paid charge-off
6. Collections or collection agencies
7. Paid collection
8. Bankruptcy liquidation
9. Repossession
10. Voluntary repossession
11. Bankruptcy
12. Judgments
13. Tax liens
14. Settled
15. Refinanced
16. Account sold or transferred
17. Account closed by merchant
18. SCNL – Subscriber cannot locate
19. Credit card lost or stolen

20.   Excessive inquiries

When you finish tagging positive and negative entries, you should have either a big ✓ or a big **X** on all the entries.

4. Recognizing the TRIO

Every entry on the credit report has three important pieces of information called the TRIO, which are the call name, the call date, and the call amount.

With your red pen you are only going to concentrate on the entries with big **X**s by underlining the following:

1.   The call name. In the public record section of the credit report, it is bankruptcy, judgments, tax liens, repossessions; in the collection section of the credit report, it is the collection agency's name or sometimes the merchant's name, and in the credit account section, it is the merchant's name or sometimes the collection agency's name.

2.   The call date. In general, the call date is the oldest date on the entry line. The call date for bankruptcy is date discharged, paid tax lien is the date paid, released tax lien is date released, judgment date is the date the case was filed. In the collection section, for Equifax it is date of delinquency, for TransUnion it is the date placed for collection, and for Experian, it is the date opened or date reported since, which ever comes first. For example, if an account on your credit report has the date opened as 2002 and date reported since as 2000, you would pick 2000, but if date opened is 1998 and date reported since is 2000, you would pick 1998. In the credit account section, it is the date opened. Do not underline date updated, date collection reported, date assigned, date of status, or date last reported. Because the collection agencies do not want this date to expire, which will force the entry to fall off from your credit report, some unscrupulous collection agents will keep changing the call date by moving it forward, a process called redating, which is illegal. The call date is very important because you do not want to underline the date when account was first opened, date of last activity, or last date reported, but the date of delinquency, which is used in calculating the cut-off date. You should underline the right call date of any entry to properly calculate the cut-off dates and waiting dates.

3.   The call amount. The call amount is very important especially, since underlining the wrong amount would end up costing you a lot of money and time. In general, it is the smallest amount on each entry line. It is the balance amount. It is very important not to throw away the last bill from a merchant, unless it is paid and you receive a zero balance bill from the merchant. Most of the amounts on the credit report are inflated sometimes with fees and penalties.

5. Calculating the Cut-off Date

Every entry that passes the cut-off date test should NOT appear on your credit report. The goal is to calculate the cut-off date and see if it came before today's date. Using the call name or the status name and the duration on the report, you will complete the cut-off form.

	Status Name	Duration on Report
1	Judgments—filed or satisfied	7 years from date filed, satisfied
2	Judgments	7 years from date of entry (NY)
3	Collections	7 years from date of delinquency
4	Charge-offs	7 years from date charged off
5	Delinquent accounts	7 years from date of delinquency
6	Late payments	7 years from date of delinquency
7	Bankruptcy Chapter 7, 11 and 13—filed or discharged	10 years from date filed or discharged
8	Tax lien filed, paid or released	10 years from date filed, paid or released
9	Other negative entries	7 years from date of delinquency

If the call date, which is the discharge date found on your credit report was 2/1/1993 you would add 10 years and the result would be 2/1/2003. Let's assume today's date is 1/1/2004, then the bankruptcy entry should not be on your credit report because the cut-off date, 2/1/2003, came before today's date, which means the entry drop-off date has come and gone. The entry should have dropped off from your credit report on 2/1/2003, which came before 1/1/2004. Since it passed the cut-off test, you would write, "Delete Outdated 2/1/2003" on the entry. You would write the credit bureau to delete the entry because it dropped off on 2/1/2003. If the cut-off date had fallen after today's date then you would calculate the waiting date.

6. Calculating the Waiting Date

This is the date you are willing to wait for the account to expire and drop from your credit report. If you don't have an impending purchase such as buying an automobile or a house, use 1 year, but if you have an impending purchase that cannot wait, use 6 months to calculate the waiting date.

You may consider the amount of the entry, also, for example, if $1,000 is going to drop off in six months or in one year, you should wait rather than write the merchants, collection agents, and credit bureaus and opening a can of worms—that is, if you don't have the cash flow to pay the $1,000.

In calculating the waiting date, if, for example, the date of delinquency was 6/1/2000 you would add 7 years to 6/1/2000 and the result would be 6/1/2007. Let's assume today's date is 8/1/2006. The delinquent account did not pass the cut off test because the cut-off date, 6/1/2007, did not come before today's date, 8/1/2006. Then we would calculate the waiting date by subtracting 1 year from the cut-off date, 6/1/2007, and the result would be 6/1/2006. The delinquent account passed the waiting date test, because the waiting date, 6/1/2006, came before today's date, 8/1/2006. That means in less than 1 year, the account would drop from your credit report. Since it passed the test, you would write, "Wait, Will Drop off 6/1/2007" on the entry.

7. Recognizing Nuisance Amounts

Now you are concentrating on the remaining negative entries with a big **X**; your goal is to have action notes on every negative entry. A nuisance amount is any negative entry with $100 or less balance. Start with the public information section, walk your way through the collection agency section, and end at the merchant account section. If you find any nuisance entry, write an action note, "Pay off now," on the entry.

8. Recognizing False Accounts

By now, you have few accounts left with a big **X** and no action notes. The next step is to look at the individual account to verify they belong to you, by looking at the merchant's name. Mistakes happen and sometimes accounts which are not yours will be listed on your credit report. Once you confirmed that a certain account listed on your credit report is not yours, you should write, an action note, "Delete False Account or Proof," on the negative entry.

Confirm the merchant's name on all third party accounts. Third-party accounts are those that are being reported to the credit bureaus by businesses other than the original merchant, especially by collection agencies. All third-party accounts will show the original merchant's name on the entry. Did you know most of your false accounts will disappear if you delete additional names that show up in the personal identification section?

9. Recognizing Duplicate Accounts

Duplicate accounts are the most common mistakes on your credit report, especially if you have a delinquent account that was sold or transferred several times. When you default on a credit account, personal loan, or hospital or utility bills, the merchant reports you to the credit bureau. After 120 days or more, the merchant will sell your account to a collection agency that will report your account to the credit bureau with a new account number listed on a separate line on your credit report. After another 120 days, the collection agency will sell your account to a second collection agency, who also reports your account to the credit bureau. In one year, you may see the same account listed three times by different companies with different account numbers.

Duplicate accounts can also occur when a national company reports your credit activities to the credit bureau and later transfers that same account to a local branch and the local branch renumbers your account and starts a new entry on your credit report. Sometimes, few dollars will be added to the original amount to make it seem like a new and different debt. If you can identify an account as a duplicate, proof of information will uncover the history of the entry. If you find any duplicate entries, write an action note, "Delete Duplicate or Proof," on

the entry. You will write to the merchant or the collection
account because it is not yours or to provide you with pro

10. Recognizing Closed Accounts

Accounts closed by merchants are considered negative v
by customers are considered positive. Look through your credit repo...
identify accounts with these comments. Underline the name of the current
holder, the name of the originator, if any, and the amount of debt. You want to
make every effort to reopen any account that says, "Closed by merchants."
Lack of activities on an account for a long period of time will cause a merchant
to close the account. Find those accounts, write an action note, "Reopen," on
all the entries. Go to the store and add merchandise to your credit account; call
the customer service at the main office from the local store with the help of the
sales person at the local store to have your account reopened. You may write a
letter to close the account at a future date after it was reopened and the account
paid off.

11. Recognizing Charge-off Accounts

Most charge-offs have been purged out of the database. As soon as you see a
charge-off on your credit report, the first thing to do is write the credit bureau
to delete the account because the account is not yours or to provide you with
proof of information. Because the account has been purged from the database,
the merchant will not respond and the credit bureau will write that the account
is deleted from your report. The second best way to handle a charge-off
account is to ask the merchant to delete, that the account is not yours or to
provide proof of information. Review how to handle this situation in the
section on dealing with the merchant. You will find out how to obtain a letter
from a merchant saying that the account can no longer be found.

Another way to handle a charge-off is to call the manager to ask if you can pay
the amount in full. If the amount is more than $200, ask for a discount or
scheduled payments, and in return, have the charge-off deleted from your
credit report. You must secure an agreement before you send any payment.
Find charge-off entries and write an action note, "Delete or Proof," on the
entries.

Recognizing Paid Charge-off Accounts

Paid charge-off is one of the worst entries on your credit report, due to the fact that you have paid off a negative entry on your credit report without first getting a deal in writing that the charge-off will be deleted after the payment from your credit report. Anytime you see a paid charge-off on your credit report, your first move is to write the credit bureau that the account is not yours or to provide you with proof of information. Most of the time, the merchant would not want to challenge it, because you've paid it off anyway. The result is the credit bureau will write you that the account is deleted from your credit report.

Another way to delete a charge-off from your credit report is to ask the merchant, in writing, to delete the charge-off because you have paid off the account. If the merchant cannot delete the entry, get the merchant to change the entry from "Paid charge-off" to "Paid as agreed," and, as usual, ask the merchant to send you a letter to that effect. If all else fails and the account is still far from the expiration date, request that the merchant delete or provide proof; therefore, you would write an action note, "Delete or Proof," on the entry.

13. Recognizing Paid Collection Accounts

This entry is like the paid charge-off. Paid collection is one of the worst entries on your credit report besides negative entries in the public information section, because it is hard to deal with the collection agencies (if the account is reported by a collection agency), much less when they have received their money with no promise of deleting the negative entry from your credit report. Now it is twice as hard to get them to talk to you. If paid collection is three years or more, it may have been purged from the database, after all, it is already paid—everyone is happy. Your first move is to write the credit bureau to delete because the account is not yours. The merchant or collection agency might not challenge it, and the credit bureau will delete. The second step is to write the merchant or the collection agency manager, and request the paid collection be changed from "Paid collection" to "Paid as agreed." The third step is to use the cut-off date and waiting date, then you would write an action note, "Wait account will drop off," on the entry.

By now, you should have red pen notations on all or most of the negative entries with big **X**s. If you still have accounts with no action notes or red pen notations, you should write, "Delete or Proof" on the entries. You will write the merchant or collection agency to delete, account is not yours or provide proof of signature, agreement, invoice, statement, and notice of delinquency. If they provide proof, you can decide to make a one-time full payment with a promise to delete now, or arrange for scheduled payments as described in dealing with merchants and dealing with collection agencies.

14. Recognizing Negative Inquiries

Inquiries are located at the bottom of your credit report. There are two parts in the inquiry section. The first part displays inquiries that affect your credit report, and the second part displays inquiries that do not affect your credit report. You should assume that all inquiries would affect your report.

Five or more entries in one calendar year are unacceptable. Unless you have a block on your report to stop inquiries for marketing and promotional purposes, many entries would come from companies you've never heard of. Look through the names of the companies listed, if inquiries are four months or fewer and you cannot verify the business name, write the company immediately to delete because you did not authorize the inquiry. According to the law, the company must delete an inquiry you did not initiate. If you initiate the inquiry, the first step is to calculate the cut-off date using two years and one year for waiting date, and write, "Delete Outdated" if expired or "Delete Wait" if it passes the waiting date test. If entry is not close to the expiration date and you cannot wait, write an action note, "Delete or Proof," on the entry.

15. Analyzing Consumer Statement

The last item on your credit report is the consumer statement. If you have written one before, it is at the bottom of the report. A consumer statement is your last resort as a rebuttal to any negative entry on your credit report. I do not recommend writing a consumer statement, unless you have exhausted all options. Your primary goal is always to delete any negative entries on your report, not to write consumer statement. However, the law allows you to write a 100-word statement.

The purpose of the statement is to shift the blame back to the merchant or the collection agency and show good cause for not paying your bill on time or at all. The most acceptable statements that neutralize any negative entries are:

1. I never ordered any merchandise from the supplier.
2. The merchandise I ordered was never received.
3. The merchandise was defective and harmful.
4. The merchandise was returned to the merchant.
5. The bill was never received due to change of address.
6. The payment I made to the merchant was returned to me.
7. The price on the bill was wrong and considered a billing error.
8. The product on the bill was wrong and considered a billing error.
9. I never knew my account was sold or transferred.

If any of these topics is applicable to you, you must write the merchant immediately as a move to inform the merchant of a "billing error" as required by law. It should not take you up to 100 words to write a professional rebuttal, as long as you are brief and precise. A professional way of writing a consumer statement is discussed in this book.

Congratulations! You have learned how to spread your report, which is one of the most important steps in cleaning your credit report. By now, you should have an action note on every entry. And because you have accurately spread your report, your job is half done.

Chapter 5

How to Spread
Your Credit Report

Common Mistakes on Credit Reports

There are two kinds of credit reports: the free report to which you are entitled once a year, and the paid report with score you get when you pay the required fees. When you ask for free information, what you get is free information—a not-so-good, watered-down version of the paid credit report. The paid credit report with score is preferable because you will compare your score before and after credit repair.

You will find the following sections on your credit report:
- Heading
- Personal Identification
- Current and Previous Addresses
- Employment and Licenses
- Public Records from Court Files
- Collections, Delinquencies, and Charge-offs
- Merchant Account Payment History
- Inquiries Initiated by You
- Inquiries Not Initiated by You

Heading. This is the credit bureau's name, address, phone number, hours of operation, and report number or confirmation number. All information in the heading section is very important, especially the confirmation number, if available. Whenever you write the credit bureau, you must give them the confirmation number so you don't have to include the actual credit report itself to save mailing cost. They use this number to track the communication between you and them. The date of the report is very important. The date is used to track and confirm changes that have been made from the last report you received. If you have to call the credit bureaus, you are limited to 60-90 days to reference the report number—and I know you will never call the credit bureaus, right? However, when you write, there is no limited number of times to use the report number, as long as the corrections you are writing about have not already been made.

There are no common mistakes in this section, but you must make sure you write the correct report number anytime you refer to it in your letter.

Identification. Most of the time, the identification section is located at the top of the report; although, sometimes, it may be displayed at the end of the report. This is where you will find your name and Social Security number. Most people do not verify their Social Security number, and because a report has a number doesn't mean the number belongs to you. The Social Security number is the only identifier that ties you to the credit report. Verify your date of birth. You must spend enough time to check out all information in the identification section to verify the report is yours.

Common mistakes in this section include listing your name with different versions and listing your date of birth incorrectly. If your name is John Doe, it will be listed as Jon Doe, John Deo, and Doe John. This kind of mistake was initially made at the merchant's office. A staff person at the computer terminal may have keyed your information in the database backward as in Doe John. Another common error is that of omission, in which the staff person typed Jon as John, or the error transposition in typing Doe as Deo. You should highlight or circle such errors for correction.

Current and Previous Addresses. Current and previous addresses should be immediately below your personal identification. If you have lived in the same house or apartment all your life, this section will have only one address. However, if you have been moving from city to city and from apartment to apartment, this section will be lengthy. There is always a mistake if your address section is very lengthy.

Common mistakes in this area are errors of omission and transposition of the street number or changing street to avenue, place, road, or parkway. Other mistakes include changing the zip code or listing the wrong city. Every time an error is made on your address, it is listed separately as a new address. You must verify your complete address. If you find any errors, just highlight or make a note for correction.

Employment and Licenses. If you never had a job, this line would be blank. If you've had several jobs, and you have used them in obtaining credit they will all be listed. You supplied most employment information that is listed on your credit report. However, there are times when employment information that doesn't belong to you is included in your report. The credit reporting system is not perfect and it is your job to find the mistakes and correct them. Also, if you have a driver's license and have used it on an application form, it may be listed on your credit report.

Common mistakes in this section are errors, including places you have never worked and a license number that is not yours. Any time you see a wrong driver's license number on your credit report, make sure you reviewed every account on your report to confirm you're not a victim of identity theft. The city and state where you have worked may not be listed correctly. If you want a certain company you have worked for to be listed on your credit report, make a note and have it listed later. For example, if you have worked for or are still working for Microsoft and you want prospective merchants to know about it, it is your job to inform the credit reporting agencies.

Public Records. Most items under this section are based on information gathered from the court records. Credit reporting agencies use their staff person or a third-party agent to collect, review, and verify public record information. Information reported in this section includes bankruptcy, foreclosures, judgments, tax liens, wage garnishments, and a host of other legal information.

Common mistakes in the public record section include accounts that are not yours, duplicate entries, and outdated entries that should have been deleted but because of incorrect date are still on your report. Another profound mistake by credit bureaus is reinsertion, the deletion of an account because of expiration or the credit bureau cannot verify with the merchant. At any time when you are not looking, the credit bureau would reinsert the negative entry. This is why you should be a part of repairing and correcting your credit report—like knowing why your account was or should be deleted. Most public record information, such as bankruptcy, would remain on your record for 10 years from the date filed. Others such as unpaid tax liens are 15 years from the date filed, paid tax liens 7 years from the date paid, and judgment debts are 7 years from the date the judgment was entered. Credit bureaus are governed by federal law—the Fair Credit Reporting Act (FCRA) and state laws.

Collections, Delinquencies, and Charge-offs. Following the public records are derogatory items. They are displayed immediately to show merchants the potential problems with your credit report. A good merchant will be excited if there are no public records and no derogatory items. But unscrupulous ones will be excited because of the huge interest payments they would gouge from you. Information in this section would include collections, delinquencies, and charge-offs. Collections are reported mostly by collection agencies; delinquencies and charge-offs are reported mostly by merchants.

Common mistakes in this section are accounts that are not yours, duplicate accounts, wrong dates, and wrong amounts on your accounts. The most profound intentional mistake by unscrupulous collection agencies is redating. Once a bad agent sees that your collection account is about to become outdated or expire and drop from your credit report, it will move the date of delinquency forward. For example, if an account was delinquent in 1990, in 1997, when it would expire and drop from your credit report, the agent would change the account and the date of delinquency from 1990 to 1997, thereby extending the account by another seven years on your credit report. By repeating the same process, the account will never be outdated and always stay on your credit report. This is against the law. Therefore, you must always keep your notice of delinquency in your credit file; hopefully, you will never receive any. I don't need to tell you what to do when you discover redating on your credit report. Hint: It's time to talk to a good lawyer and laugh all the way to the bank. Another common mistake would be a collection agency reporting an account and later selling it to another agency. The new collection agency would report the same account under its name with a new date; thereby, making it a duplicate account on your credit report.

Merchant Accounts Payments History. This is the main body of your credit report, which lists all the accounts you currently have and how good or bad your payment records are. It would list open and closed accounts with information such as paid satisfactorily, 30, 60, 90, or 120 days past due. The only comments you want to see on your credit report in this section are paying as agreed, pay as agreed, paid as agreed or paid satisfactorily.

Common mistakes you would find in the merchant accounts payment history section include accounts that are not yours, duplicate accounts, incorrect date an account was opened, incorrect account balances, or positive status accounts that were never reported. Duplicate accounts occur when your account is being reported by one merchant, and later sold or transferred to another merchant. The new merchant would give your account a new number and start reporting the same account as a separate and new account. As described in the previous sections, redating and reinsertion are very rampant in this section also. The Fair Credit Reporting Act allows credit bureaus to list positive status accounts on your credit reports indefinitely. However, the credit bureaus may delete them after 10 years if you are not watching.

Inquiries Initiated by You. Every time you apply for credit, you have initiated a credit inquiry on your credit report. Sometimes, you will see an AM or AR on your credit report in the inquiries section. These are inquiries made by your current creditors. They want to see if there is any adverse information on your report that would alert them to be careful in extending you credit in the future. Bankruptcy, tax liens, and other legal notices would cause the creditor to restrict or refuse future credit lines. If your credit limit is high, credit card companies will review your credit report every month or at least every three months. From time to time, you will see words such as ACIS and Update. These allow access to your credit report by the credit bureau. When you write the credit bureaus their access to your file is recorded, and when the access results in changes in credit report, it is noted as "Updated."

Common mistakes in this section include not removing inquiries after the two-year period. You should review inquiries in your report and match them with new accounts. Sometimes, inquiries can stay longer than the two years required by law because the merchant or the credit bureau documented an incorrect date. If you look closely, you might even find inquiries from a company you have never heard of or done business with.

Inquiries Not Initiated by You. If you opt out of marketing promotions, you should have no entry in this section. You opt out of credit bureau databases for unsolicited marketing promotions to deny a credit bureau the right of selling your information to the telemarketing companies. When you have a block, few people can get into your report without your knowledge. In this section, you would see words like PRM, promotional inquiries.

Common mistakes in this section are listing the names of companies you have never heard of or done business with and outdated inquiries that should have been dropped. Watch for these kinds of mistakes. Other mistakes are recording the wrong date, thereby, extending the life of the inquiry.

A Sample of a Credit Report

Report Date: January 1, 2004

Confirmation #999125125475
Please address all future
correspondence to:

Credit Bureau Services
123 Cunning Rd
Allen, TX 70007

Sample Credit File

Personal Identification Information
John Deo
132 Adam Lane
Dallas, TX 75141

Social Security #123-45-6789
Date of Birth: January 1, 1900

Previous Address(es):
456 Frenzy St., El Paso, TX 79998
P.O. Box 123, Richardson, TX 75122

Last Reported Employment: Sales Manager, World Wide Sales, Inc.

Public Record Information
Bankruptcy Filed 1/93; Northern Dist. Ct; Case ID 543HC21 Liab $21,425; Personal;
Individual; Discharged 2/1/96: Assets $21,425

Satisfied Judgment Filed 01/90; Dallas CTY; Case or Other ID 987654
Defendant John Doe; Amount $5,251; Plaintiff XYZ Real Estate;
Satisfied 3/90; Verified 08/90

Tax Lien Filed 03/94; Dallas CTY; Case or Other ID 12345; Amount $25,825 Class-State;
Released 07/95; Verified 07/95

Collection Agency Account Information
ABC Collection Agency 1-800-123-4567 Reported 10/2000; Delinquent 1/2000, Assigned
10/2000 Client Health Hospital; Amount $526; Unpaid; Balance $526; Date of Last Activity
1/2000; Individual Account; Account Number 123456

National Collection Agency 1-800-222-4567 Reported 10/2005; Delinquent 6/2000,
Assigned 10/2000 Telephone of America; Amount $50; Unpaid; Balance $50; Date of Last
Activity 10/2005; Individual Account; Account Number TX45678

Department Store of USA 1-877-211-4500 Reported 1/2003; Delinquent 6/1995, Balance $1,589; Date of Last Activity 1/2003; Individual Account; Account Number 125TX45678.

Credit Account Information

Comp Name (1)	Acct Num (2)	Whose Acct (3)	Date Open (4)	Months Rev (5)	Date of Default (6)	High Credit (7)	Term (8)	Balance (9)	Past Due (10)	Pay Status (11)	Date Last Updated (12)
XYZ	1234	J	1/00	24	NA	$5,000	$150	$2,500	$0	Paid as agreed	1/03
Auto	5678	I	6/00	10	4/01	$25,748	$259	$11,859	$259	30 days past	4/01
Bank	9876	A	12/97	20	NA	$1,457	$25	$0	$0	Paid as agreed	5/98
Auto	6459	I	5/92	60	6/94	$19,477	$350	$4,520	$700	60 days past	6/94

Previous Payment History; 1 Time 30 days late; 1 Time 60 days late
Previous Status: 6/94 – I1; 7/94 – I1; 8/94 – I1

Inquiries Initiated by You

1/27/1998 AR Bank of America 4/1/2000 AR Department Store
1/7/2001 AR Auto Company   6/16/2003 World Finance Company
3/17/2002 Credit Bureau Disclose   8/20/2003 USA Bankcard

Inquires Not Initiated by you

PRM Bank Card Company
ACIS Department Store
PRM Auto Store
PRM Furniture Company
PRM Marketing Services Company
INQ Real Estate Services

Consumer Statement (100 words)

A typical consumer statement: "On February 12, 1994, I bought a kitchen set from Department of USA, and the order was received on March 24, 1994. When the kitchen set was plugged into an electric socket, it sparked and no longer worked. The next day, March 25, 1994, the merchandise was returned to the company with a return receipt requested. After receiving the merchandise, Department of USA continued to bill me for the defective product. The company did not reply to my registered mail and request for proof of information."

Explanation of the credit account information section listed above is as follows:

1- Credit grantor reporting the information
2- Account number reported by the credit grantor
3- See explanation on whose account
4- Month and year the credit grantor opened the account
5- Number of months account payment history has been reported
6- Date of last payment or date of default
7- Highest amount charged or the credit limit
8- Number of installments or monthly payment
9- The amount owed as of the date reported
10- The amount past due as of the date reported
11- Status of account
12- Date of last account updated

Whose Account for #3

Indicates who is responsible for the account and the type of participation you have with the account.

J = Joint
I = Individual
U = Undesignated
A = Authorized User
T = Terminated
M = Maker
C = Co-Maker/Co-Signer
B = On Behalf of Another Person
S = Shared

Status – Type of Account

O = Open (entire balance due each month)
R = Revolving (payment amount variable)
I = Installment (fixed number of payments)

Explanation of Inquiries

PRM – For promotional purposes, this type of inquiry means that only your name and address were given to a credit grantor so they could offer you an application for credit. PRM inquiries remain for 12 months.

AM or AR – For review purposes, these inquiries indicate a period review of your credit history by one of your creditors. AM and AR inquiries remain for 12 months.

ACIS or Update – These inquiries indicate a credit reporting agency's activity in response to your contact with them for either a copy of your credit file or a request for research.

Credit Bureau, ACIS, Update and INQ – These inquiries do not appear on credit files businesses receive, only on copies provided to you.

Medical and Health inquiries are not displayed to the creditors, and are not used to calculate your credit score.

Consumer's Accurate Information

Before we start spreading, let's look at the consumer's true information. We will then take this accurate information and match them with what the credit bureau is reporting on the consumer's credit report. True and accurate consumer's information is as follows:

1. We assume today's date and the date on the report is 1/1/2004
2. Consumer's name is John Doe
3. Date of birth 1/1/1900
4. Social Security number is 123-45-6789
5. Address: 123 Adam Lane, Dallas, TX 75114
6. Previous address: P.O. Box 123, Richardson, TX 75122
    John Doe has only one address and one P.O. Box number.
7. Employment: Sales Manager, World Wide Sales, Inc.
8. Bankruptcy was filed on 1/1/93; liability amount was $21,452.

9. Judgment was satisfied on 3/30/90.
10. Tax lien was released on 7/10/95.
11. John Doe has never been to Health Hospital and did not owe $526.
12. When John called ABC Collection Agency, he found out he was being mistaken as one John Deo who lives at 456 Frenzy Street.
13. John owes Telephone America $50.
14. John owes Department of USA $1,589.
15. John has never filled out an application with World Finance Company and USA Bankcard.

With the following facts, we are going to spread John Doe's credit report using the spreading steps we discussed earlier. You should make a copy of the sample credit report above—it will be a lot easier for the spreading process.

Let's Spread a Credit Report

You have seen a sample of how a credit report looks. The actual credit report format may change from time to time from this sample. Changing the format of the credit report is at the discretion of the credit bureau. However, every credit report must contain the basic information as displayed in the included credit report sample. We are going to take the following spreading steps one by one and see how to spread a typical credit report. Let's review the spreading steps once again:

1. Proofread the personal identification section
2. Tag positive accounts with check marks
3. Tag negative accounts with **X** marks
4. Recognize the TRIO on the negative accounts
5. Calculate cut-off on the negative accounts
6. Calculate waiting period on the negative accounts
7. Recognize nuisance dollar amounts, if any
8. Recognize false accounts not belonging to you, if any
9. Recognize duplicate accounts, if any
10. Recognize closed accounts by merchants, if any
11. Recognize charge-offs, if any
12. Recognize paid charge-offs, if any

13.   Recognize paid collections, if any
14.   Recognize negative inquiries, if any
15.   Review consumer statement
16.   Remove negative accounts

Proofread the Personal Identification

With the red pen in hand, you will proofread the personal identification section.

- Circle John Deo because the right name is John Doe not Deo. Write beside the name, "Please correct."
- Circle 75141, the right zip code is 75114, and write, "Please correct."
- The Social Security number is correct so put a ✔, meaning you've confirmed your Social Security number. This is very important. Without the right Social Security number, the entire report is not yours.
- Under previous address section, circle 456 Frenzy Street, El Paso, TX 79998 and write, "Please delete." John did not live anywhere except Dallas, Texas.

Tag Positive Accounts

Tagging the entries is one of my favorite activities. With the red pen still in hand, you will underline any of the following status name: paying as agreed, pay as agreed, paid satisfactorily, current, current no late payments, paid/never late, paid, paid closed, paid closed by customer; and then put a big ✔ on the left margin of the credit report. Let's begin. Since you are tagging positive, skip the public record and the collection agency sections and go to credit account information section, because all the entries in public record and collections sections are negative entries. Underline the following beside these positive accounts:

- For the XYZ account, underline "pay as agreed" and put a big ✔ on the left margin beside XYZ.
- For the bank account, underline "pay as agreed" and put a big mark ✔ on the left margin beside Bank.

Tag Negative Accounts

Like tagging the positive entries, with the red pen and starting with the public record section, you will underline any of the following status names: For judgments—satisfied or filed; for bankruptcy—discharged or filed; for tax liens—paid, released, or filed; and for other accounts—delinquent, past due, or charge-off, etc. Then put a big **X** on the left margin of the credit report. When tagging the negative accounts, you will start with the public record and walk your way through the collection information section, where most of the entries are negative accounts.

Public Record Information

- For the bankruptcy entry, underline "Discharged" and put a big **X** on the left margin beside Bankruptcy.
- For the judgment entry, underline "Satisfied" and put a big **X** on the left margin beside Judgment.
- For the tax lien entry, underline "Released" and put a big **X** on the left margin beside Tax Lien.

Collection Agency Account Information

- For the ABC Collection account, underline "Delinquent" and put a big **X** on the left margin beside ABC Collection.
- For the National Collection account, underline "Delinquent" and put a big **X** on the left margin beside National Collection.
- For the Department Store of USA account, underline "Delinquent" and put a big **X** on the left margin beside Department Store of USA.

Credit Account Information

- For the auto account 5678, underline "30 days past" and put a big **X** on the left margin beside Auto 5678.
- For the auto account 9876, underline "60 days past" and put a big **X** on the left margin beside Auto 9876.

Recognize the TRIO on Negative Accounts

Recognizing the TRIO is the one of the most important steps in the spreading process. This time you will concentrate on the negative accounts only or accounts with a big **X**. Underlining the right information will determine if an account should have been deleted from your credit report. It makes a big difference if you are to arrange for monthly payments on an account or wait it out in six months to drop from your credit report. That's how important the TRIO is.

With the red pen you are will underline the Call Name, the Call Date, and the Call Amount. How to find these has been described in Chapter 4, "Spread Your Credit Report."

Public Record Information

- For the bankruptcy entry, underline Bankruptcy, 2/1/96, and $21,425.
- For the judgment entry, underline Judgment, 3/90, and $5,251.
- For the Tax Lien entry, underline Tax Lien, 07/95, and 25,825.

Collection Agency Account Information

- For the ABC, underline ABC Collection Agency, 1/2000, and $526.
- For the National, underline National Collection Agency, 6/2000, and $50.
- For the Department Store, underline Department Store of USA, 6/95, and $1,589.

Credit Account Information

- For the Auto account 5678, underline Auto 5678, 4/2001, and $259.
- For the Auto account 6459, underline Auto 6459, 6/94, and $700.

Calculate Cut-Off Date on Negative Accounts

With the call name, call date, and status name, you will calculate the cut-off date on the negative entries with big **X** on them. You will assume that you received your credit report on the report date, which is January 1, 2004 (see the date on the report above). You will be calculating the cut-off date based on the duration of each entry. The duration is the number of years the negative entry must stay on your credit report and then drop off or be deleted by the credit bureau.

Remember for the cut-off test to pass, the cut-off date must come before today's date, which is 1/1/2004. If any of the entries pass the cut off test, you will write the following, "Request bureau to delete" on the entry.

Public Record Information

- For the Bankruptcy entry, duration is 10 years from date discharged.
  The underlined 2/96 plus 10 makes the cut-off date 2/2006.
  Cut-off date, 2/2006, did not come before today, 1/1/2004. Test failed.
- For the Judgment entry, duration is 7 years from date satisfied.
  The underlined 3/90 plus 7 makes the cut-off date 3/97.
  Cut-off date, 3/97, came before today, 1/1/2004. Test passed.
  Circle the X, put a big ✔ by the X and write, "Credit bureau to delete."
- For the Tax Lien entry, duration is 10 years from date released.
  The underlined, 07/95, plus 10 makes the cut-off date 7/2005.
  Cut-off date, 7/2005, did not come before today, 1/1/2004. Test failed.

Collection Agency Account Information

- For the ABC Collection, duration is 7 years from date of delinquency.
  The underlined, 1/2000, plus 7 makes the cut-off date 1/2007.
  Cut-off date, 1/2007, did not come before today, 1/1/2004. Test failed.
- For the National Collection, duration is 7 years from date of delinquency.
  The underlined, 6/2000, plus 7 makes the cut-off date 6/2007.
  Cut-off date, 6/2007, did not come before today, 1/1/2004. Test failed.
- For the Department Store of USA, duration is 7 years from date of delinquency.
  The underlined, 6/95, plus 7 makes the cut-off date 6/2002.
  Cut-off date, 6/2002, came before today, 1/1/2004. Test passed.

Circle the **X**, put a ✔ by the **X** and write, "Credit bureau to delete."

<u>Credit Account Information</u>

- For the Auto account 5678, duration is 7 years from date of delinquency.
  The underlined, 4/2001, plus 7 makes the cut-off date 4/2008.
  Cut-off date, 4/2008, did not come before today, 1/1/2004. Test failed.
- For the Auto account 6459, duration is 7 years from date of delinquency.
  The underlined, 6/94, plus 7 makes the cut-off date 6/2001.
  Cut-off date 6/2001 came before today 1/1/2004. Test passed.
  Circle the **X**, put a ✔ by the **X** and write, "Credit bureau to delete."

Calculate the Waiting Date on Negative Accounts

The waiting date is how long you are willing to wait for the entry to expire, which will force the credit bureaus to delete it from your credit report. If you don't have a pressing need, you may use one year. Also, depending on the amount, it is worth it to wait for $5,000 to expire in one year, unless you have the cash flow to pay the $5,000.
In this exercise, you will be using one year. You will concentrate on the accounts that failed the cut-off date test from the previous exercise. The waiting date is calculated by subtracting one year from the cut-off date.

Remember for the waiting date test to pass, the waiting date must come before today's date, which is 1/1/2004. If any of the entries pass the waiting date test, you will write the following, "Will drop off" on the entry.

<u>Public Record Information</u>

- For the Bankruptcy entry, cut-off date is 2/2006. The cut-off date 2/2006 minus 1 makes the waiting date 2/2005.
  Waiting date, 2/2005, did not come before today, 1/1/2004. Test failed.
- For the Tax Lien entry, cut-off date is 7/2005.
  The cut-off date 7/2005 minus 1 makes the waiting date 7/2004.
  Waiting date, 7/2004, did not come before today, 1/1/2004. Test failed.

Because the amount is $25,825, you should wait. Circle the **X**, put a big ✓ by the **X** and write, "Will drop off 7/2005."

<u>Collection Agency Account Information</u>

- For the ABC Collection, cut-off date is 1/2007.
  The cut-off date 1/2007 minus 1 makes the waiting date 1/2006.
  Waiting date, 1/2006, did not come before today, 1/1/2004. Test failed.
- For the National Collection, cut-off date is 6/2007.
  The cut-off date 6/2007 minus 1 makes the waiting date 6/2006.
  Waiting date, 6/2006, did not come before today, 1/1/2004. Test failed.

<u>Credit Account Information</u>

- For the Auto account 5678, cut-off date is 4/2008.
  The cut-off date, 4/2008, minus 1 makes the waiting date 4/2007.
  Waiting date, 4/2007, did not come before today, 1/1/2004. Test failed.

Recognize Nuisance Amounts

In recognizing nuisance amounts, you are looking for $100 or less or any amount, depending on your cash flow. You are willing to pay right away to have the negative entry deleted from your credit report. It is very annoying to have $10 from a hospital bill pull 50 or more points from your credit report.

But before you send any money, make sure the collection agent or the merchant will sign a letter of agreement (a sample letter is provided) that he or she will delete the $10 negative entry from your credit report within 30 days of payment. Start with the public record information section and looking at the call amount you have underlined already. We are concentrating on small amounts that failed the cut-off date test—not the waiting date test—because you don't want to wait for one year or six months. You want to pay it off now—right away to get it off your credit report.

If you find any nuisance amount on your credit report, write "Pay off now" on the entry.

Public Record Information

- No nuisance amount found.

Collection Agency Account Information

- For the National Collection, the call amount is $50
Circle the **X**, put a big ✔ by the X and write, "Pay off now."

Credit Account Information

- No nuisance amount found.

Recognize False Accounts

When John received his credit report called ABC Collections; he was told the account belonged to him because he lived at 456 Frenzy Street. He was being mistaken with one John Deo who is living at that address. In actuality, it was John Deo who went to Health Hospital and who owed the $526, not John Doe.

John told the collection agency he never lived at that address, the issue was cleared, and the collection agency promised to remove the negative entry from John Doe's credit report. Circle the **X**, put a big ✔ by the **X** and write, "Agency will delete."

Public Record Information

- No false accounts found

Collection Agency Account Information

- John Doe found out the ABC Collection is a false account on his credit report and the collection agency promised to delete it. Put a big ✔ on the entry and write, "Agency to delete."

Credit Account Information

- No False accounts found

Recognize Duplicate Accounts

John has only three accounts to deal with and all his effort is concentrated on these three accounts. There are no duplicate accounts on his credit report. Most duplicate accounts will come from a merchant reporting an account and selling or assigning the same account to a collection agency, who reports the same account to your credit report. In most instances the amount will be inflated to make it seem as if it were a different account. If John had found any duplicate accounts, he would have written, "Delete duplicate account" on the entry.

Public Record Information

- No duplicate accounts found

Credit Account Information

- No duplicate accounts found

Recognize Closed Accounts by Merchant

Closed accounts by merchant may mean fraudulent activities have taken place on the account and the merchant decided to close it. It might also mean that the customer was delinquent and the merchant decided to close the account and report the balance to the credit bureau or sell the account to a collection agency. Whatever the reason, closed account by the merchant is seen by other merchants as a negative entry on your credit report. Most accounts that are reported as closed by merchant are also reported by a collection agency or are listed as a delinquent account. Always look for duplicate entries any time you see closed by merchant account. This is one of those tips credit repair software will never teach you.

There are no closed accounts by merchant; otherwise, John would have re-opened the account by working with the merchant. If John had found any duplicate accounts, he would have written, "Reopen account" on the entry.

Public Record Information

- No closed accounts by merchant found

Credit Account Information

- No closed accounts by merchant found

Recognize Charge-off Accounts

Charge-off account is almost like the duplicate account. The merchant will charge-off or write off the account from its books, and, at the same time, sell or assign the same account to a collection agency, who will duplicate the entry on your credit report.

There are no charge-off accounts; otherwise, John would have worked with the merchant to pay off the amount (if small) or wait for it to drop off on its own.

Public Record Information

- No charge-off accounts found

Credit Account Information

- No charge-off accounts found

Recognize Paid Charge-off Accounts

Paid charge-off is almost like charge-off, but in this case, you paid the merchant or the collection agency after it was charged off without asking the merchant or the collection agency to sign an agreement to delete after you paid the account in full.

As explained earlier, this is one of the worst entries on your credit report, because now nobody will talk to you or agree to delete the negative entry because the account is closed. One of the best actions is to ask the merchant or the collection agency to change the account to "Paid as agreed," or you might want to wait for the account to drop off on its own.

There are no paid charge-off accounts; otherwise, John would have worked with the merchant to change it to "Paid as agreed."

Public Record Information

- No paid charge-off accounts found

Credit Account Information

- No paid charge-off accounts found

Recognize Paid Collection Accounts

Paid collection is almost like the paid charge-off, but different because the paid collection is being reported by a collection agency not a merchant. You have paid the collection agency without getting a written agreement as explained previously. If a merchant would work with you to change a paid charge-off to paid as agreed, most collection agencies will not even talk to you much less agree to change the paid collection to paid as agreed.

You do not want to change paid collection to paid as agreed because you don't want the word collections on your credit report. The word collection is regarded as a negative remark on your credit report. The best action is to wait for it to drop off on its own. With what you know now, you will never allow a paid collection account on your credit report.

There are no paid collection accounts; otherwise, John would have written, "Wait it out" on the entry.

Public Record Information

- No paid collections accounts found

Credit Account Information

- No paid collections accounts found

Recognize Negative Inquiries

Negative inquiries should have dropped from your credit report because of the statute of limitation of two years the law allows inquiries to stay on your credit report. If you review your report and find any entries from longer than two years ago, you should write the credit bureau to delete it from your credit report.

Another type of negative inquiry is the one that is made by companies without your consent. Credit bureaus will tell you it does not affect your points. Don't listen to anyone; ask the company to remove it from your report because it is limiting you from making your legitimate inquiries. Since making too many inquires in one year is negative, the unsolicited inquiries are an intrusion.

Let's look at some of the inquiries:
1/27/1998 Bank of America plus 2 years is 1/27/2000
1/27/2000 came before 1/1/2004 and should be deleted from credit report.

1/7/2001 Auto Company plus 2 years is 1/7/2003
1/7/2003 came before 1/1/2004 and should be deleted from credit report.

6/16/2003 World Finance Company is an unsolicited inquiry and should be deleted by World Finance Company, unless you want to wait for it to drop off in two years.

8/20/2003 USA Bankcard is an unsolicited inquiry and should be deleted by USA Bankcard, unless you want to wait for it to drop off in two years.

John has some unsolicited inquiries and the best way to handle these is to opt out from the credit bureau database as discussed in this book. The credit bureau is the one that sold your information to the marketing companies.

Review Consumer Statements

Unfortunately, John wrote a long but very unprofessional consumer statement that is still in his credit report. However, after completing the cut-off test, you found out the Department Store of USA account passed the cut-off test. That account was supposed to have been deleted from your credit report as it is has been on your credit report for more than the 7 years allowed by law.

Any time an entry in the credit report is deleted, the accompanying consumer statement must be deleted by the credit bureau. John should write on the consumer statement, "Credit bureau to delete."

Remove Negative Accounts

We have marked negative accounts with a big **X**, except three accounts. Let's review what to do with them:

Public Record Information

- For the Bankruptcy entry, cut-off date is 1/2006.

Since the bankruptcy has only one year after the waiting date to drop from the credit report, John should wait to let it drop off. Another option is to request that the credit bureau delete the entire entry because the amount it was reporting was incorrect. The credit report says $21,425 when the actual liability amount was $21,452. According to the law, little data entry mistakes like these qualify the entry to be deleted from your credit report. Because the amount is large, it's better to wait. Circle the **X**, put a big ✓ by the **X** and write, "Will drop off 2/2006."

Credit Account Information

- For the Auto account 5678, cut-off date is 4/2008 with 30 days past due.

Since the auto account is still open, John should ask for a one-time courtesy to have the automobile company delete the negative entry from his credit report. If you have been paying on time after you missed one or two payments, good company are willing to over look it and delete it from your report. You must ask in writing to the director of the finance department. Circle the **X**, put a ✓ by the **X** and write, "Delete one time courtesy."

Congratulations! You have dealt with every negative account on your credit report and have made the necessary remarks on how to remove them from your credit report. This is, by far, one of the most important steps in repairing your credit report—like they say, "The rest is history."

Chapter 6

Set up Your Credit Score Binder

Set up Your Credit Score Binder

Your credit score binder is an organized filing system called the communication tracking system. This tool is the engine that drives the whole credit repair machine and is very powerful in preventing scheduled tasks from falling through the cracks. With this system every credit report document is located in the blink of an eye. At any second, you know exactly when a reply from a merchant, collection agency, and credit bureau will reach you. You would not know the importance of the binder until you start looking for letters from credit bureaus, merchants, and collection agencies. However, with this proprietary system in your hands, your organizational skill is second to none.

The purpose of the communication tracking system is to present irrefutable legal documentation on your credit history and to methodically organize your credit information in an easy-to-reach filing system. There are 10 tabs in the communication tracking system binder:

1.   List of accounts tab
2.   Communication tab
3.   Annual credit report tab
4.   Equifax tab
5.   Experian tab
6.   TransUnion tab
7.   Other credit reporting agency tab
8.   Merchants tab
9.   Collections tab
10.   Legal tab

1. List of Accounts Tab

List of account section has three pages: list of negatives, list of positives, and list of cut-offs. These pages allow you to display every negative, positive, and cut-off date entry on your credit report, in summary fashion.

List of negatives. By listing the negative entries, you will be able to tell which accounts to target immediately for payoff because the amount is too small to be dragging down your credit score. It is presented in a way you can tell instantaneously which credit bureaus is reporting which negative account. This is very important because sometimes one or two credit bureaus might not be reporting on every negative entry. Your task is to use your credit report to complete the list of negatives. Use the following steps to complete the list of negatives:

1. Open the list of negatives page, then open your Equifax credit report and find the first negative entry

2. Enter Call name, which is one of the TRIO from the credit report, for example write Bankruptcy or Tax Lien.

3. Enter the Call date, which is one of the TRIO. For judgments—date of filing, for released tax liens—date released, for paid tax liens—date paid, and for other negative accounts—date of delinquency.

4. Enter the credit bureau's name. Since you are looking at an Equifax report, write EQ and a slash, because you are going to see if another credit bureau is also reporting that same entry

5. Enter the Call amount, one of the TRIO, the amount of judgment for public entry, amount of delinquency for collection, and amount of delinquency for other negative accounts.

6. Enter the objective. The objective of most negative entries is to be deleted. For paid collections—paid as agreed, for paid charge-off accounts—paid as agreed. After you have written the objective, put a small ✔ on the entry on the credit report.

7. Repeat the above process for every negative entry on the Equifax credit report by putting a small ✔ on the report and when you have completed the process, you should have tiny ✔ on all negative entries.

8. Open your Experian credit report and see if Experian is reporting the first entry on the list of negatives. If Experian is reporting the first entry on the list, write EX after the slash and put a small ✔ on the Experian

report. If Experian is not reporting the first entry on the list, go to the next entry until you have reviewed all entries. After you have completed the process on the Experian credit report, there should be a small ✓ on every entry.

9.   Open your TransUnion credit report and see if TransUnion is reporting the first entry on the list of negatives. If TransUnion is reporting the first entry on the list, write TU after the slash and put a small ✓ on the TransUnion report. If TransUnion is not reporting the first entry on the list, go to the next entry until you have reviewed all entries. After you have completed the process on the TransUnion credit report, there should be a small ✓ on every entry.

Following is a sample form provided for your use:

List of Negatives

Call Name	Call Date	CRA	Call Amt	Objective
1. Bankruptcy	2/1/1993	EQ/EX/TU	$21,425	Delete
2. ABC Coll	6/1/1995	EQ/TU	$526	Delete

3. _____

4. _____

5. _____

6. _____

7. _____

8. _____

9. _____

10. _____

11. _____

12. _____

13. _____

14. _____

15. _____

16. _____

List of positives. The process of listing the negatives is the same as listing the positives. List of positives is used to find out which credit bureau is not reporting a particular positive account. If a credit bureau is not reporting a positive entry, your credit score with that credit bureau should be lower. You will write a letter to a credit bureau to add your positive account thereby increasing your credit score.

Some merchants may choose to report to all three credit bureaus and others may choose to report to only one or two credit bureaus. Your task is to use your credit report to complete the list of positives. Use the steps for the list of negatives as previously described and the following explanation of the headings to complete the list of positives:

- Call Name is the same as in the list of negatives. The name of the merchant is who reported the negative entry with the credit bureau.

- Date in this case is the date the account was first opened not the call date. Every entry has the date the account was originally opened.

- Credit Reporting Agency is the same as in the list of negatives, the credit bureau that is showing the positive entry.

- Payment is the monthly payment you agreed to make to the merchant during the time you signed the agreement and this should match what is on the credit report.

- Balance is the current balance on the account. This amount is listed under the column heading Balance on your credit report.

- Credit Limit is the total amount you borrowed or in the case of credit cards or revolving accounts, the highest amount you can charge.

Following is a sample form provided for your use:

List of Positives

Call Name	Date	CRA	Payments	Balance	Credit Limit
1. XYZ	1/1/2000	EQ/EX	$150	$2,500	$5,000
2. Auto	6/10/2000	EX/TU	$259	$11,859	$25,748

3. _____

4. _____

5. _____

6. _____

7. _____

8. _____

9. _____

10. _____

11. _____

12. _____

13. _____

14. _____

15. _____

16. _____

List of cut-offs. Your credit report may have some expired entries on it. The cut-off date will pinpoint exactly which entries on your report have expired and should have been deleted from the report. If you still have an entry that is not expired, the next question is, "Am I willing to wait for six months or one year for the entry to expire and drop off on its own?" This is the intent of calculating the waiting period. After completing the waiting period, you will be able to tell which entries will be dropping off in the future and when. Your task is to use your credit report to complete the list of cut-offs. Use the following steps to complete the list of cut-offs:

1.   Go to the list of negatives tab in your binder and copy the names of the originators from the list of negative entries to the list of cut-offs.

2.   Go to the credit report and copy the call name, the call date, and the status name, where they already have been underlined.

3.   Find the number of year associated with each status name. Use the following list to find the number of years (for example, with bankruptcy, discharged is a status name and 10 is the number of years to add to the call date):

      a.   Bankruptcy discharged, 10 years from the date discharged
      b.   Bankruptcy, if not discharged, 10 years from date filed
      c.   Tax lien paid, 10 years from the date paid
      d.   Tax lien released, 10 years from the date released
      e.   Tax lien, if not paid or released, 10 years from the date filed
      f.   Judgments satisfied, seven years from the date satisfied
      g.   Judgments, if not satisfied, seven years from date filed or entered
      h.   Judgments, five years from the date of entry (NY residents)
      i.   Collections, seven years from the date of delinquency
      j.   Charge-offs, seven years from the date of charge-off
      k.   Delinquents, seven years from the date of delinquency
      l.   Late payments, seven years from the date of delinquency
      m.   Negatives, seven years from the date of delinquency

4.   Add the number of years to the call date.

5.   Write the result in the cut-off date column.

6.   Add one year or six months to the cut-off date.

7.   Write the result in the waiting date column.

Following is a sample form provided for your use:

List of Cut-offs

 Call Name   Status Name Call Date   Cut-off Date Waiting Date

1. Bankruptcy Discharge 2/1/93 + 10 yrs = 2/2003 – 1 yr = 2/2002

2. ABC Coll Delinquent 6/1/95 + 7 yrs = 6/2002 – 1 yr = 6/2001

3. _____

4. _____

5. _____

6. _____

7. _____

8. _____

9. _____

10. _____

11. _____

12. _____

13. _____

14. _____

15. _____

2. Communications Tab

The communications tab has two pages—written and oral. The written page identifies the key contents and purpose of your letter, while the oral communication identifies the person you spoke to, the date, time, and the agreement. Another keynote of this section is the date of expected reply. To find the date of expected reply, simply add one month to the date you sent the letter and write the results under the heading, "Approximate date of exp. reply." In a split second, you will know when a particular reply should reach you and your next action. The purpose of the communication section is to make sure all communications are fully documented for future reference. Your task is to make sure blank copies of written and oral communication pages are present in this section. Following is the explanation of the written communication headings:

1. Company is the merchant you are dealing with right now; the company might not be the originator of the entry.

2. Purpose is exactly what you want the company to do.

3. Date sent is the stamped date from the post office, if sent by certified mail, or date mailed, if sent by ordinary mail.

4. Date of expected reply is one month added to the date you sent the letter.

5. Add one month and 15 days if you sent additional information to the credit bureau within the 30-day period.

Oral contracts are hard to prove but your chances of proving your case are high if you have a diary or formal journal like the one below. Following is the explanation of the oral communication headings:

1. Company is as in written communication list.

2. Purpose is as in written communication list.

3.   Staff person is the name of the person you spoke with.

4.   Date/Time is today's date and time you spoke with the staff person.

5.   You must get some information from the staff person such as the date to call back if documents or agreement are not received.

Following are sample forms provided for your use:

Written Communication

	Company	Purpose	Date Sent	Approximate Date of Exp. Reply
1.	ABC Coll	Delete or Proof	1/1/2004 + 1 month	= 2/1/2000
2.	Equifax	Delete Expired	2/1/2004 + 1 month	= 3/1/2000

3. _____

4. _____

5. _____

6. _____

7. _____

8. _____

9. _____

10. _____

11. _____

12. _____

13. _____

14. _____

15. _____

16. _____

<u>Oral Communication</u>

<u>Company</u>	<u>Purpose</u>	<u>Staff</u>	<u>Date/Time</u>	<u>Promises</u>
1. ABC Coll	Correction	John D	1/18/2004 2:30 PM	Will report paid As agreed 2/15
2. Auto Comp	Proof	Kay #4158	7/1/2004 11:15 AM	Will send Proof 7/21

3. _____

4. _____

5. _____

6. _____

7. _____

8. _____

9. _____

10. _____

11. _____

12. _____

13. _____

14. _____

15. _____

16. _____

3. Annual Credit Report Tab

This section is reserved for the annual credit report and all three-in-one credit reports like the ones you would receive from VantageScore or other credit delivery companies. You may get your credit score from a source like the VantageScore; which is a company created by Equifax, Experian, and TransUnion to sell three-in-one credit reports. Also, you can buy a three-in-one report on the Internet. This is a credit report that pulls all the activities of the three major credit bureaus—Equifax, Experian, and TransUnion—into one report. I do not recommend the three-in-one report, but if you are in a hurry and want a report to look at right away, it is good place to start. I strongly recommend dealing with VantageScore or each credit bureau separately, rather than the Internet credit report sources. Your task is to insert your annual credit report or the three-in-one credit report in this section as you receive them.

4. Equifax Tab

This section is reserved for credit reports and documents you receive directly and individually from Equifax. The purpose of this section is to track every communication with Equifax in an organized manner. You should file your letters and subsequent credit reports on top as you send and receive them—the most recent information is always on top. Your task is to insert your credit report and letters from Equifax on top of each other as you receive them.

5. Experian Tab

This section is reserved for letters, credit reports and subsequent credit reports you receive directly from Experian. Your task is to insert your credit report and letters from Experian on top of each other as you receive them.

6. TransUnion Tab

This section is reserved for letters, credit reports and subsequent credit reports you receive directly from TransUnion. Your task is to insert your credit report and letters from TransUnion on top of each other as you receive them.

7. Other Credit Bureaus Tab

From time to time, you may run into credit reports from your local credit bureaus or other national credit bureaus not related to the three major credit bureaus. If you have any account with credit monitoring companies such as credit watch companies, this section is reserved for credit reports from those companies. Your task is to insert your credit report and letters from other credit bureaus on top of each other as you receive them.

8. Merchants Tab

Sometimes, you will have to communicate with different merchants who have reported negative entries on your credit report. This section would help you to be very organized in such a way that in a moment's notice you know the date, time, and the staff person you spoke with last. As you get organized, you will be amazed how information flows from date to date. Your task is to insert your letters from merchants on top of each other as you receive them, and, if possible, to create separate tabs if you have two or more merchants.

9. Collection Agencies Tab

As the name implies, this section is reserved solely for the collection agencies. If possible, make a tab for each collection agency you have on the list of negatives. It is vitally important to go straight to a tab and locate all the documents when replying to collection agencies—your binder will make this possible. Your task is to insert your letters from collection agencies on top of each other as you receive them, and, if possible, to create separate tabs if you have two or more collection agencies.

10. Legal Tab

You may not be dealing with the FTC, your state Attorney General, the BBB, or a business attorney; however, I want you to be fully equipped should this section become an option. Your task is to create a legal tab for the FTC, Attorney General, BBB, and other legal representatives and insert your letters from them on top as you receive them.

Chapter 7

Working with Credit Bureaus

Writing an Unprofessional Letter

The first clue to the credit bureaus that you're unprofessional or you don't know your rights is your proof of information letter. If your letter is not precise about what you want, credit bureaus will immediately reply that they cannot delete a factual statement from your credit report. The credit bureaus do not change information on your credit report; rather, they change the information on your credit report as ordered by their "masters," namely the merchants and collection agencies. Your letter must be specific and bold. If the credit bureaus detect rambling, ambiguity, or weakness in the tone of your letter, they will send you a computer-generated letter. You recognize a computer-generated letter when it slightly answers your question and includes a host of other answers you never thought of or asked.

Anytime you receive a computer-generated letter it's a tip off that:

a.   You were not specific in your letter to the credit bureau.
b.   The credit bureau is buying time to investigate your case.
c.   You are asking them to do what you should have done yourself.
d.   They are testing your knowledge level on what to do next.

Most consumers would freeze once they receive a computer-generated letter. You should reply immediately and this time, be very specific: I want you to delete the bankruptcy entry; it is inaccurate. ABC Company collection account is outdated. XYZ Stores account is not mine. Delete account number 123456—I have never been delinquent.

They will reply back that they are investigating the case and will report back to you as soon as the investigation is completed for which they have only 30 days to reply and 45 days if you send additional information within the 30-day period. After the merchant or the collection agency receive a verification letter from the credit bureau, the merchant or collection agency sends a notice back to the credit bureau that says something such as, "Account is verified as accurate." Is this how to accurately investigate and verify an account? The credit bureau is just doing their job; it is not their account, their low credit score, or their high interest rate—but yours! Immediately, the credit bureau will send you a summary page of your credit report that says, "Account is verified as accurate." Ninety-nine percent of the time, people go directly to the credit bureaus to dispute every negative entry on their reports. This is unprofessional and is a tip-off to the credit bureaus that you don't know what you're doing; therefore, all you'll get is a computer-generated letter.

You do not go to court, stand before the judge and say that you're innocent without any evidence or proof. What you would be doing here is demanding evidence and proof from merchants and collection agencies, which the law allows you to collect from them, to prove the account is yours or the amount is correct. Although you can consult a professional legal attorney, you have to investigate your account not the credit bureau. I have made it easy for you to do so and not to pay exorbitant fees to the credit repairing companies or credit repairing software companies.

Six Types of Professional Letters

In correcting your credit report, there are six specific issues on your report you should only deal with directly with the credit bureaus and not with a merchant or collection agency:

1.   Correcting personal identification because
   a.   Information is not correct
   b.   Information is not yours
   c.   Information is not included
   d.   Information is obsolete

2.   Correcting public information because
   a.   Information date is not correct
   b.   Information amount is not correct
   c.   Information is not yours
   d.   Information is obsolete

3.   Deleting outdated account entries on your report.

4.   Deleting entries in compliance with merchant's letter.

Thirty days after you receive a letter from a merchant on an agreement to delete an entry, you should write the credit bureau to inquire if the account is actually deleted. Ask the credit bureau to send you an updated copy of your credit report. If the entry is still on your report, send a copy of the letter from the merchant and ask the credit bureau to make the correction. The credit bureau will call the merchant to verify your letter and make the necessary correction and forward you an updated version of your credit report.

5.   Deleting entries in compliance with collection agency's letter.
Thirty days after you receive a letter from the collection agency on an agreement to delete an entry, you should also write the credit bureau to confirm the account is deleted. If the account is not deleted, forward a copy of the letter to the credit bureaus, and ask them to delete the account and forward to you an updated copy of your credit report.

6.   Deleting at-large subscribers' negative entries.
Sometimes you will write to a merchant or collection agency and your letter will be returned back to you. At this time, you must confirm the address on the envelope with the address you received from the credit bureaus. If the address is the same, write to the credit bureau to delete accounts, enclosing a copy of the envelope from the post office. Because all addresses and phone numbers of subscribers came to you in writing (not over the phone) from the credit bureau, it cannot say you had the wrong address, and any investigation would reach the same conclusion.

Correcting Personal Information Entries

Now, we are going into the letter-writing phase, let me remind you there are six areas in which you should go to the credit bureau, also known as the credit reporting agency directly: Personal information, public information, outdated accounts, complying with merchant, complying with collection agency, and deleting at-large subscriber entries.

Almost all credit reports have incorrect information in the personal identification section. Maybe your name is listed several times with one of them spelled incorrectly, or your address is listed several times for places you've never lived. Look very carefully, you will find incorrect information in the identification section. You don't need your previous addresses listed if you have lived in your current address for more than five years.

We are going to use two examples: A Letter to the Credit Reporting Agency to Correct Personal Information and a Letter to the Credit Reporting Agency to Delete Outdated Entry, to see step by step, from start to finish how to write and receive these letters from the credit bureaus. You will be able to use these letters to write any letters to the credit bureaus. You should treat personal information the same way you treat public information in terms of sending and receiving letters from the credit bureaus.

The personal identification information is actually supplied by you, but because the report does not display the actual source, it is assumed the origination is the credit bureau and, therefore, shoulders the burden of proof of information, unless it provides the source and phone number.

Letter to the Credit Reporting Agency to Correct Personal Information

After you spread your credit report and find errors in the personal identification, write the credit bureau to correct them. Credit bureaus are cooperative in correcting personal identification information, after all, it is to their best interest to update and carry the correct information about you. Your letter to the credit reporting agency about personal information should focus on the following possible problem areas:

- Information is not correct
- Information is not yours
- Information is not included
- Information is obsolete

You should write the credit bureau, for example, to delete information because an entry it is not yours or to provide proof of information and sources of information, including addresses and phone numbers. Your letter to correct your personal identification information should include the following requests and facts:

1.   Write your letter to the manager of customer relations.
2.   Disclose that you received your credit report from the credit bureau.
3.   Give the credit report number.
4.   List the information you would like to be corrected.
5.   Ask that an updated copy to be sent to you.
6.   Send by certified mail only without return receipt requested and type the certified mail number on your letter

Sample Letter to Correct Personal Information

John Doe
1234 Adam St.
Dallas, TX 75111

January 1, 2004

Manager Customer Services
Equifax
P.O. Box 740241
Atlanta, GA 30374
Certified Mail #1234 5678 9123 4567 8912

Dear Manager:

I've just received my credit report bearing the number 999125125475, and noticed the following personal identification information is incorrect:

1.   My name is John Doe not John Deo.
2.   My address is 1234 Adam Street not 1234 Adam Lane.
3.   I have never lived at 456 Frenzy Street, El Paso, TX 79998.

Please delete and correct these entries immediately or send me proof of information including signatures, agreements, invoices, statements, and sources of such information, including addresses and phone numbers to determine the accuracy and completeness of information presented on my credit report.

Your earliest reply is greatly appreciated.

Sincerely,

John Doe

What Reply to Expect from the Credit Bureau

After you have requested some personal identification be corrected on your credit report, any one of the following could happen:

- Return to sender
- The credit bureau did not reply.
- The credit bureau wants more information.
- The credit bureau replied and corrected all the entries.
- The credit bureau replied and corrected some or none of the entries.

1. Return to sender. With credit bureaus, you will not be getting any return to sender unless your address is incorrect. Double check your address, if is wrong resend your letter.

2. The credit bureau did not reply. Most of the time, the credit bureau will correct your report and send you an updated copy, unless they do not receive your letter. Make sure the address you copied from the Internet is correct. If after 30 or 45 days, you send additional information and get no reply, write a follow-up letter to the president of customer services, enclose a copy of your previous letter, and send it return receipt requested. Include the fact that it has been more than 30 days since you wrote your first letter.

3. The credit bureau wants more information. If you receive this kind of letter, find out exactly what the credit bureau wants and send that and nothing more.

4. The credit bureau replied and corrected your report. This is what happens most of the time.

5. The credit bureau replied and corrected some or none of the entries. There should be no problems in correcting your personal identification information. If the credit bureau insists the information is correct and should not be changed, write a follow-up letter and demand a proof of information letter immediately and include the following requests and facts:

a. Address it to the vice president of customer services.
b. Include the credit report number.
c. Acknowledge the fact that you have received your credit report.
d. Request proof of information on the incorrect entries.
e. List only the incorrect information.
f. Send your letter certified mail and return receipt requested and type the certified mail number on the letter.

Sample Follow-up Letter to
Correct Information

John Doe
1234 Adam St.
Dallas, TX 75111

January 1, 2004

Vice President, Customer Services
Equifax
P.O. Box 740241
Atlanta, GA 30374
Certified Mail #1234 5678 9123 4567 8912
Return Receipt Requested

Dear Vice President:

It has been more than 30 days since you refused to correct personal identification information on my credit report. My credit report number is 999125125475.

Please correct these errors or, as required by law, I'm formally requesting for proof of signature, agreements, invoices, statements, and a description of the procedure used to determine the accuracy and completeness of the information, including the business name and address of any furnisher of information contacted in connection with such information and the telephone number of such furnisher. You have 15 days to comply with the following requests:

1.   My name is John Doe not John Deo.
2.   My address is 1234 Adam Street not 1234 Adam Lane.
3.   I have never lived at 456 Frenzy Street, El Paso, TX 79998.

Your immediate reply is greatly appreciated.

Sincerely,

John Doe

Letter to the Federal Trade Commission for Compliance

If the credit bureau does not correct personal identification information after your second letter and a total of 60 days have passed, it's time to report it to the FTC, the Attorney General of your state, and your local BBB. The purpose of writing to the FTC and the Attorney General is compliance. You are asking the government to ask the credit bureau to comply with the law. The purpose of writing the BBB is for business and community awareness.

You can file your complaint with the FTC at www.ftc.gov. Click "File a Complaint" at the top of the home page. You will be taken to the form for submission. You can also file your complaint in writing, which is better, so you can customize your complaint. The best way to find the current address of the FTC is to click "About FTC" on their Web site.

Federal Trade Commission
600 Pennsylvania Ave., N.W.
Washington, DC 20580

When you write the FTC, you want to include the following in your letter:

1. Title your letter Credit Report Enforcement.
2. You are filing a complaint against a credit bureau for not correcting personal identification information, according to the law.
3. You have written two letters to the credit bureau.
4. Enclose copies of the two previous letters.
5. Ask the FTC to open an investigation into the matter.
6. Include your name, address, Social Security number, and telephone number.
7. Send your letter certified mail and return receipt requested and type the certified mail number on your letter.

Sample Letter for Compliance

John Doe
1234 Adam St.
Dallas, TX 75111

January 1, 2004

Federal Trade Commission
600 Pennsylvania Ave., N.W.
Washington, DC 20580
Certified Mail #1234 5678 9123 4567 8912
Return Receipt Requested

Dear Commissioner:

Credit Report Enforcement

I am filing a formal complaint against (XYZ Credit Bureau). I have asked the credit bureau to correct personal identification information on my credit report, as required by law. It has been more than 60 days since the credit bureau refused to comply with the law, by distributing a false credit report on my behalf. I am losing thousands of dollars in interest payments due to a low credit score.

I am enclosing the previous letters I wrote to the credit bureau for your review and action. My Social Security number is 123-45-6789 and my telephone number is (123) 456-7890. Please open an investigation into this matter.

Your earliest reply is greatly appreciated.

Sincerely,

John Doe

Letter to the Attorney General for Compliance

Send a similar letter to the Attorney General of your state. To find the address and phone number, look in the white pages of your phone book under Government—State. Call the number and get the address of the person or department in charge of credit bureau and credit reporting complaints. When you write to the Attorney General of your state, you may include the following in your letter:

1.   Title your letter Credit Report Enforcement.
2.   You are filing a complaint against a credit bureau for not correcting personal identification information entry, according to the law.
3.   You have written two letters to the credit bureau.
4.   Enclose the two previous letters in your envelope.
5.   Ask the Attorney General to open an investigation into the matter.
6.   Include your name, address, Social Security number, and telephone number.
7.   Send your letter certified mail and return receipt requested and type the certified mail number on your letter.

Sample Letter for Compliance

John Doe
1234 Adam St.
Dallas, TX 75111

January 1, 2004

Attorney General, State of Texas
P.O. Box 12548
Austin, TX 78711
Certified Mail #1234 5678 9123 4567 8912
Return Receipt Requested

Dear Commissioner:

Credit Report Enforcement

I am filing a formal complaint against (XYZ Credit Bureau). I have asked the credit bureau to correct personal identification information on my credit report, as required by law. It has been more than 60 days since the credit bureau refused to comply with the law, by distributing a false credit report on my behalf. I am losing thousands of dollars in interest payments due to a low credit score.

I am enclosing the previous letters I wrote to the credit bureau for your review and action. My Social Security number is 123-45-6789 and my telephone number is (123) 456-7890. Please open an investigation into this matter.

Your earliest reply is greatly appreciated.

Sincerely,

John Doe

Letter to the Better Business Bureau for Compliance

Write a simple letter to the BBB and enclose the previous letters to the credit bureau. The best way to contact the local BBB, is online using the following steps:

1. Visit www.search.bbb.org/search.html.
2. You are taken to the BBB Information System page.
3. To search for Experian in the search box, click in the Name box and type Experian. Then click the Search button.
4. You are taken to the Database Search Results page.
5. On the left column, click on Experian and select the name of your state in the address or click the headquarters.
6. You will be taken to the code window. A different code is displayed each time the window is opened. Type the code in the Enter Code box, and click Submit.
7. You will be taken to the BBB Reliability Report page. Read the Customer Experience paragraph for satisfactory or unsatisfactory remarks.
8. Click the Contact Us button to write the address of your local BBB for when you send your letter.

The second best way to contact the BBB is to look in the white pages of your local telephone book. You may also call the 1 800 number information line. The following steps may be used to send your letter to the BBB:

1. Write to the director of your local BBB.
2. Title your letter Credit Report Enforcement.
3. You are filing a complaint against a credit bureau for not correcting personal identification information, according to the law.
4. You have written two letters to the credit bureau.
5. Enclose the two previous letters in your envelope.
6. Ask the BBB to open an investigation into the matter.
7. Include your Social Security number, and telephone number.
8. Send the letter by certified mail with return receipt requested.

Sample Letter for Compliance

John Doe
1234 Adam St.
Dallas, TX 75111

January 1, 2004

The Better Business Bureau of Dallas County
1234 Any Street
Anytown, TX 75000
Certified Mail #1234 5678 9123 4567 8912
Return Receipt Requested

Dear Commissioner:

                    Credit Report Proof of Information

I am filing a formal complaint against (XYZ Credit Bureau). I have requested
the credit bureau to correct personal identification information on my credit
report, as required by law. It has been more than 60 days since the credit
bureau refused to comply with the law, by distributing a false credit report on
my behalf. I am losing thousands of dollars in interest payments due to a low
credit score.

I am enclosing the previous letters I wrote to the credit bureau for your review
and action. My Social Security number is 123-45-6789 and my telephone
number is (123) 456-7890. Please open an investigation into this matter.

Your earliest reply is greatly appreciated.

Sincerely,

John Doe

Letter to the Credit Reporting Agency to Delete Outdated Entry

We have looked at how to correct personal identification information, now let's look at how to request the credit bureau to delete an outdated or expired negative entry from your credit report. Most people have outdated entries on their credit report, and these mistakes are dragging their credit score down. By reviewing your credit report and doing something about it, you become one of the few credit repair elite.

You would need to write a letter to the credit bureaus listing the accounts that should have been deleted from your credit report. These accounts are easily taken care of by the credit bureaus because of the legal consequence of showing an outdated negative entry on your credit report. Deleted outdated negative entries are brought back to life and reported to merchants on three specific occasions: if you are applying for credit worth more than $150,000, if you are applying for life insurance worth more than $150,000, or seeking employment with salary worth more than $75,000.

The process of deleting an outdated entry is similar to correcting personal identification information. You write the credit bureau to delete the outdated entry or provide proof of information. If you do not receive a satisfactory reply in 30 days, send a follow-up letter, demanding that the credit bureau delete the outdated entry or provide proof of information. After another 30 days following the date of your follow-up letter, file a formal complaint with the FTC, Attorney General, and BBB.

One of the most important facts about spreading your report is finding out that your report has obsolete or expired entries. Remember, you may uncover more obsolete entries after you have received proof of information and proof of delinquency, if the date of delinquency on the proof is different from the date of delinquency on the credit report. You will discover that some of the accounts were actually redated by merchants and collection agencies. At this point, you should waste no time in writing the credit bureau. After all, you don't need to remind the credit bureaus to do their jobs. All outdated and expired entries should drop automatically from your credit report, and your credit report should be authenticated by the credit bureau before publication and distribution to their customers. Actually, when the credit bureau receives the proof of information, they will quickly delete the entry and reply to you that the entry has been deleted. I'm letting you know in case they forget and send you outdated date of delinquency on the proof of information. Your letter should include the following facts and requests:

1.   Address it to the manager of customer service.
2.   Acknowledge the fact that you have received your credit report.
3.   List the names of outdated accounts that need to be deleted.
4.   Include the report number and request that your report be updated and a copy sent to you.
5.   State the fact that it is against the law to distribute your credit report with outdated accounts.
6.   Request that the accounts be deleted immediately or for you to be sent verifiable documents that the account is not outdated.
7.   Send your letter certified mail without return receipt requested and type the certified mail number on the letter.

Sample Letter to Delete Outdated Entry

John Doe
1234 Adam St.
Dallas, TX 75111

January 1, 2004

Manager Customer Services
Equifax
P.O. Box 740241
Atlanta, GA 30374
Certified Mail #1234 5678 9123 4567 8912

Dear Manager:

I've just received my credit report bearing the number 999125125475, and noticed the following accounts are outdated and should have been deleted:

1.   Satisfied Judgment 987654
2.   Department Store of USA account # 125TX45678
3.   Auto account # 6459

Please delete and correct these entries immediately or send me proof of information, including signatures, agreements, invoices, statements, and sources of such information, including addresses and phone numbers to determine the accuracy and completeness of information presented on my credit report.

Your earliest reply is greatly appreciated.

Sincerely,

John Doe

What Reply to Expect from the Credit Bureau

After you have requested that an outdated account be deleted from your credit report, any one of the following could happen:

- Return to sender
- The credit bureau did not reply.
- The credit bureau wants more information
- The credit bureau replied and deleted all outdated entries.
- The credit bureau replied and deleted some or none of the entries.

1.   Return to sender. By now, you know what to do with return to sender letters from the credit bureau. Check the address or use a different address and resend your letter. The credit bureau will reply next time because you have the right address.

2.   The credit bureau did not reply. Most of the time, the credit bureau will reply to your inquiries unless they do not receive your letter. Make sure the address is correct. After 30 days, write a follow-up letter to the vice president of customer services, enclose a copy of your previous letter, and send your letter return receipt requested. Include the fact that it has been more than 30 days since you wrote your first letter.

3.   The credit bureau wants more information. If they want more information, they may enclose the dispute forms. Check of the last item, "Others," and write, "See attached letter" on the line. Enclose your letter and provide the information they are looking for. Be sure to send what they are looking for and nothing more.

4.   The credit bureau replied and deleted all outdated entries, as requested. Great! Review the updated copy thoroughly and make sure the right accounts were deleted, and your credit score was increased.

5.   The credit bureau replied and deleted some or none of the entries. There should be no problems in deleting the accounts because you calculated the cut-off date based on the call name and the call date from your

credit report. You should write for proof of information immediately and include the following requests and facts:

a.   Address it to the vice president of customer services.
b.   Include the credit report number.
c.   Acknowledge the fact that you have received your credit report.
d.   You want the following information deleted or the following proof of information forwarded to you proof of signature, agreements, invoices, statements, and notices of delinquency.
e.   List only the outdated accounts that need to be deleted.
f.   Include the fact that obsolete accounts are costing you thousands of dollars due to a low credit score.
g.   Send your letter certified mail and return receipt requested and type the certified mail number on the letter.

Follow-up Letter to Delete Outdated Entry

John Doe
1234 Adam St.
Dallas, TX 75111

January 1, 2004

Vice President Customer Services
Equifax
P.O. Box 740241
Atlanta, GA 30374
Certified Mail #1234 5678 9123 4567 8912
Return Receipt Requested

Dear Vice President:

It has been more than 30 days since you refused to delete obsolete entries on my credit report. My credit report number is 999125125475.

Please delete the outdated information or, as required by law, I'm formally requesting proof of signature, agreements, invoices, statements, and a description of the procedure used to determine the accuracy and completeness of the information, including the business name, address and telephone number of any furnisher of information contacted in connection with such information. You have 15 days to comply with the following requests:

1. Satisfied Judgment ID 987654
2. Department Store of USA account # 125TX45678
3. Auto account # 6459

I have enclosed your dispute form for your reference. Your immediate reply is greatly appreciated.

Sincerely,

John Doe

Formal Complaint to the
Federal Trade Commission

If after your follow-up letter, and 60 days of not getting a satisfactory result, send a letter of formal complaint to the FTC, the Attorney General of your state, and your local BBB.

When you write the FTC, you want to include the following in your letter:

1.   Title your letter Credit Report Enforcement.
2.   You are filing a complaint against a credit bureau for not correcting personal identification information, according to the law.
3.   You have written two enclosed letters to the credit bureau.
4.   Ask the FTC to open an investigation into the matter.
5.   Include your name, address, Social Security number, and telephone number.
6.   Send your letter certified mail and return receipt requested and type the certified mail number on the letter.

Sample Formal Complaint

John Doe
1234 Adam St.
Dallas, TX 75111

January 1, 2004

Federal Trade Commission
600 Pennsylvania Ave., N.W.
Washington, DC 20580
Certified Mail #1234 5678 9123 4567 8912
Return Receipt Requested

Dear Commissioner:

Credit Report Enforcement

I am filing a formal complaint against an (XYZ Credit Bureau). I have requested that the credit bureau delete an obsolete account from my credit report, as required by law. It has been more than 60 days since the credit bureau refused to comply with the law by distributing a false credit report on my behalf.

I am enclosing the previous letters to the credit bureau for your review and action. My Social Security number is 123-45-6789 and my telephone number is (123) 456-7890. Please open an investigation into this matter.

Your earliest reply is greatly appreciated.

Sincerely,

John Doe

Formal Complaint to the Attorney General

Write a similar letter to the Attorney General of your state. To find the address, look in the phone book or call any lawyer and ask for it.

Formal Complaint to the Better Business Bureau

Write a letter to the BBB and enclose the previous letters to the credit bureau. Just a reminder, the BBB is not going to force any credit bureau to comply the way the FTC and Attorney General would, but just to help publicize the credit bureau as a bad business to the community.

Requesting a Final Credit Report

After you have deleted most of the negative entries on your credit report, wait 30 days before requesting your credit report with score. Enclose the correct fees if you're requesting credit report with score. Your credit score will definitely increase when compared to the original score before you started the repair process.

You must clean your credit report and receive a high score before applying for a large amount of credit for a purchase such as buying a house or a new car. The best time to start cleaning your credit report is six months or more before applying for the credit. In essence, the best time to start cleaning your credit report is when you don't need credit—and the time is NOW! Before requesting your final credit report, you should have the following enhancement accounts on your report:

1.   At least a minimum personal loan account paid off from a bank that reports to three major credit bureaus paid off.

2.   At least a minimum personal loan account paid off from a credit union that reports to three major credit bureaus.

3.   At least a minimum line of credit on a Visa credit card with 90%-100% available credit balance.

4.   At least a minimum line of credit on MasterCard credit card with 90%-100% available credit balance.

5.   At least a minimum line of credit on a department store revolving account with zero current balance outstanding.

6.   A minimum line of credit on a computer store revolving account with zero current balance outstanding.

7.   A minimum line of credit on furniture store installment credit, paid off, with zero current balance outstanding.

8.   A minimum line of credit on jewelry store installment credit, paid off, with zero current balance outstanding.

Before you open any of these accounts, ask for the minimum amount to open the account, and apply for that amount. You must open an account where you ordinarily shop and avoid companies that sell for higher prices than competitors or charge higher fees than others. Open these accounts only when it is what your cash flow will allow. This is just a menu of what to choose from and see reflected on your credit report. Find other lines of credit, such as automobile or mortgage loans.

Review your final credit report and make sure you have the following positive rating entries:

• Paying as agreed
• Pays as agreed
• Paid satisfactorily
• Current
• Current no late payments
• Paid/Never late
• Paid
• Paid closed

- Paid closed by customer

Review your final credit report and make sure you have very few or none of the following negative rating entries:

1.   Current – 30, 60, 90, 120+ days late
2.   Late payment
3.   Delinquent
4.   Charge-off
5.   Paid charge-off
6.   Collections or collection agencies
7.   Paid collection
8.   Bankruptcy liquidation
9.   Repossession
10.   Voluntary repossession
11.   Bankruptcy
12.   Judgments
13.   Tax liens
14.   Settled
15.   Refinanced
16.   Account sold or transferred
17.   Account closed by merchant
18.   SCNL – Subscriber cannot locate
19.   Credit card lost or stolen
20.   Excessive inquiries

You must keep your final report with the new score in a very safe place and carry it with you when applying for credit. Do not show it to anyone, not even the merchant, unless you find a deleted entry on your credit report that the merchant just received from the credit bureau.

Opting Out of Secret Inquiry

If you have an excellent credit report and are getting junk mail and crank calls, the credit bureaus have sold your information to the marketing companies. The

credit bureaus do not make money by only selling you the credit report with score. They make more money by selling information about you.
If you want to exclude your name from the credit bureau database for the purposes of selling your credit information to anyone—the law has given you the power to do that. If you request your credit report from the credit bureaus and used the sample letter included in this book, you will receive "A Summary of Your Rights under the Fair Credit Reporting Act." The law makes the credit bureaus print and distribute the consumer rights to whomever asks for it. You may not receive this information if you do not ask for it.

Since 2004, you may choose to exclude your name from credit reporting agency lists for unsolicited credit and insurance offers. Creditors and insurers may use file information as the basis for sending you unsolicited offers of credit or insurance. Such offers must include a toll-free phone number for you to call if you want your name and address removed from future lists. If you call, you must be kept off the lists for two years. If make a request, complete and return the credit reporting agency form provided for this purpose, you must be taken off the lists indefinitely. The word "indefinitely" may change to five years in the future.

Did you read your rights? If you call, you must be kept off the lists for two years. If you want to be kept off indefinitely, you must put it in writing. A sample copy of a letter you can send to the three major credit bureaus is provided below.

Since 2006, you may limit "prescreened" offers of credit and insurance you get based on information in your credit report. Unsolicited "prescreened" offers for credit and insurance must include a toll-free phone number you can call if you choose to remove your name and address from solicitors' lists. You may opt-out with the nationwide credit bureaus at 1-888-5-OPTOUT (1-888-567-8688. The best way to remove your name permanently from the credit bureaus' database is to write them directly with the sample letter below. When you receive your credit report, you will see somewhere on your credit report, especially in the personal identification information section, "Alert(s): File Blocked for Promotional Purposes." If you do not see this on your credit report, you've not been excluded yet from unsolicited offers.

You should send this request by registered mail only; return receipt is not necessary. Staple your registered mail receipt to a copy of your letter and file this in a credit report binder.

Sample Letter to Opt Out of Inquiry

John Doe
1234 Adam St.
Dallas, TX 75111

January 1, 2004

Manager Customer Service
Equifax
P.O. Box 740241
Atlanta, GA 30374
Certified Mail #1234 5678 9123 4567 8912

Dear Manager:

On my credit report, I have discovered many inquiries, which I did not initiate. Therefore, I want to permanently exclude my name from the credit reporting agency lists for unsolicited credit and insurance offers.

Please do not to share my credit information with anyone without expressed written authorization from me and I do not expect to see any inquiries on my credit report that I did not originate.

Your earliest reply is greatly appreciated.

Sincerely,

John Doe

Using a Statement to Neutralize a Negative Entry

The consumer statement is one of my favorite areas to work on during the credit repairing process. Your goal is never to write a consumer statement, but rather delete or correct negative entries on your credit report. There are times when a merchant or a collection agency has proof that you owe money and the worst part, the incident just happened last year—not even close to the cut-off date. I do not recommend writing a consumer statement at all, because your objective is first to delete every negative entry. However, if you want to apply for credit as soon as possible and cannot wait, a consumer statement is a powerful tool you can use to neutralize any negative entry on your credit report and render it ineffective. This is one of the hidden secrets you will use so that a merchant won't count a negative entry against you. It's now your word against theirs and whoever is before the judge (the merchant), wins the case.

If you don't have a consumer statement against a negative entry, the merchant, especially an auto dealership, will throw a hospital bill you have not paid, from two years ago, in your face. But with the consumer statement at the bottom of the report, the merchant will not bring up negative entry. If the dealership or anyone mentions anything about that particular negative entry, say, "The company does not have proof the account is mine, they will soon delete it off my credit report." You're off the hook—case closed!

The primary purpose of a consumer statement is to fight back. You are shifting the blame back to the merchant—the account is not yours. You would not want to see more than two consumer statements on your credit report; you want to concentrate on the ones that are hard to remove. The following are the most acceptable reasons for consumer statements:

- I never ordered any merchandise from the supplier.
- The merchandise I ordered was never received.
- The merchandise was defective and harmful.
- The merchandise was returned to the merchant.
- The bill was never received due to change of address.
- The payment I made to the merchant was returned to me.
- The price on the bill was wrong and considered a billing error.

- The product on the bill was wrong and considered a billing error.
- I never knew my account was sold or transferred.

Do not write the consumer statement if you are going to say that it was your fault. What good is it to write that kind of statement? Statements like: I lost my job, I was sick, or I was in the hospital—are unacceptable! How would you feel if you were the merchant, and you were reading statements like that? I know the merchant would be thinking, "I don't want to be your next victim." Here is another one, "The dog ate my bill and I could not mail my check to the merchant." This is not the forum to plead for forgiveness for your previous misfortune. You may use the following steps to write your letter to the credit bureaus:

1.   Make your statement as brief as possible, you may not need all 100 words allowed by law.
2.   Your statement is a rebuttal to tell your side of the story; state a correct reason for not paying the bill.
3.   Do not write the statement if you are going to say it's your fault.
4.   Send your statement only to the credit bureaus that are reporting the account as a negative entry. Refer to the list of negatives to find out which credit bureau is reporting the account as negative.
5.   Tell the credit bureaus that you want your statement to be reported "as is" without alterations.
6.   Include your Social Security number and your date of birth.
7.   Request an updated copy of your credit report after the statement is included in your report.
8.   Send your letter certified mail with return receipt requested and type the certified mail number on your letter.

A Professional Consumer Statement

Let us look at a typical statement from a consumer who has no idea how to write a professional consumer statement. He wrote, "On January 10, 2000, I ordered one book for $50, but ABC Company sent me two books and charged me $100. I promptly returned one of the books with registered mail number 1234 5678 9123 4567 8912 to the company with a payment of $50 for the one book I kept. I have made several calls to the company with no help from the management. I have formally sent a registered letter demanding proof of information on the debt; to date, I have not heard from ABC Company. I do not think I should pay for merchandise I do not have. Any good company should be able to credit my account in other to keep a loyal and repeat customer like me."

Instead of writing the whole story of what happened, which nobody has time to read, a more professional consumer statement is: "This account is not mine; ABC Company could neither verify nor send me proof of information on this account, as required by law."

You may use any of the following professional statements that suits your need:

1.   "This is not my account. ABC Company could neither verify nor provide proof of information, as required by law."

2.   "This is not my account. ABC Company could not verify, validate, or provide proof of debt, as required by law."

3.   "This is not my account. ABC Company could not provide documentary evidence of obligor's indebtedness, as required by law."

Sample Letter to Add Consumer Statement

John Doe
1234 Adam St.
Dallas, TX 75111

January 1, 2004

Manager Customer Service
Equifax
P.O. Box 740241
Atlanta, GA 30374
Certified Mail #1234 5678 9123 4567 8912

Dear Manager:

Please insert the following consumer statement with reference to ABC
Company account number 555551414125:

"This is not my account. ABC Company could not verify, validate, or provide
proof of debt, as required by law."

My date of birth is January 1, 1900. Copies of Social Security card and utility
bill are enclosed for proof of identity. My consumer statement should be
reported "as is" without alterations and changes. I would like to have an
updated copy of my credit report.

Your earliest reply is greatly appreciated.

Sincerely,

John Doe

Chapter 8

Working with Merchants

Requesting Proof of Information

After you've received your credit report, unless your account has been transferred to a collection agency, your first step is to contact the merchant who reported the negative entry. Most counselors and books would tell you to take your problem to the credit reporting agencies. After wasting six to nine months writing back and forth with credit bureaus, you would finally be referred to the same merchant. The tool in your hands is designed to show you the short cuts to positive results with minimal effort.

For a delinquent account that is still open with the merchant, your primary goal is to ask for a one-time courtesy to delete a negative entry or change it to "pay as agreed" if the account is actually yours. If you do not succeed, your next step is to request proof of information. The purpose is to find out everything about the account, especially the date of delinquency, and to see if the account is expired or due to expire from your credit report. You must trace a negative entry to see if it is being reported on all three major credit reports. Sometimes, an account may not be reported to the three major credit bureaus—Equifax, Experian, and TransUnion. Experian would not include the last four digits of your account number, claiming it is for your security. If you do not have the right account numbers, a merchant will find it very difficult to help you. Therefore, look at all three credit reports for complete and accurate account numbers before contacting the merchant.

You need to know there are two types of merchants you could be facing during your credit repairing process:

1.   The first merchant is one with whom you currently have an open account, and are still making payments to—month after month. This merchant needs your money to be in business; his or her survival depends on your monthly payments. You are most likely going to work with this merchant, especially if you have been a good customer. You are a good customer if you have been buying from this merchant and have been making your payments on time. You are also a good customer if you have concentrated buying power with a merchant (i.e., buying all your clothes from one department store or all your groceries on one credit card). Volume purchase is a powerful bargaining tool.

When you direct any complaint and the merchant looks at your history and sees strong purchasing power or high volume purchases, your requests are treated with utmost priority and with positive answers—all the time—guaranteed!

2.   The second type of merchant is one with whom you have a closed account. If your account was closed because you have finished paying on a particular debt, you are still considered a good customer. However, if your account was closed because you failed to make payments, you are not considered a good customer.

Your strategy in dealing with a merchant would depend on the amount that is showing up on a negative entry on your credit report. In requesting proof of information when working with a merchant, your relationship may be classified into any one the following scenarios:

1.   Open account
        Volume buyer

2.   Open account
        No volume buyer

3.   Closed account
        Volume buyer

4.   Closed account
        No volume buyer

First category. If your account falls in the first category, where your account is still open and you are a volume buyer, with late payment, the process of removing a negative entry on your credit report is fairly easy.

You should write to the manager of customer services, not the supervisor. Make sure the customer service department is at the address where you are sending your letter. If possible, call the company using the phone number on your bill. In most cases, your bill will contain a phone number where you can reach customer services with any questions you may have. Call to make sure you get the correct and complete address of the merchant before sending your proof of information letter.

Customers that fall in the first category should send their follow-up letter by certified mail only without return receipt. Staple the certified mail receipt to a copy of the letter in your file.

Your letter should have a friendly tone, because you are a good customer, who is expecting the merchant to keep your business by meeting your demands. In your letter, you should bring up the fact that you have been a good customer and want to continue to be one—for a long time. You can go the extra mile by congratulating the customer service department on their superior services. Your letter should say something such as, "You are reporting to the credit bureau that I was delinquent on my account. I can't recall being late. Please delete this negative entry or send me a copy of the original notice of delinquency."

Second category. If you fall in the second category, where your account is still open, and you are not a volume buyer with a late payment, you should use a different strategy in dealing with a merchant.

The first thing you should do is increase the volume of your business by concentrating your buying power with this merchant. You have heard about one-stop shopping, and the purpose of having different merchandise under one roof is to capture every dollar a household spends each month of the year. For example, you could buy clothes, shoes, kitchen items, bedding items, furniture, and entertainment items all from one store, instead of buying all these items from different businesses.

If you are going to buy those items anyway, you might as well buy them from someone who could help increase your credit score. I do not recommend over-spending your budget to increase your credit score. A customer can use one-stop shopping as a bargaining chip when it comes to correcting an error on a credit report.

Your letter should be directed to the vice president of customer services, if there is one. If there is no vice president of customer services, write and address your letter to the vice president anyway. The intent is to make sure the highest-ranking employee in the organization handles this case. Customers who fall in the second category should send their first letter by certified mail, returned receipt requested. Staple your certified mail receipt and the signed returned receipt card to a copy of the letter in your file.

The content of your letter should be friendly and informative. You want to extend your thanks to the wonderful customer service department. Also, inform the president that you have been a good customer and a quick review of your account would show evidence of increasing activities. The most important part of your letter is your request to delete or send you proof of information on a delinquent account. "You are reporting to the credit bureau that I was delinquent on my account. I can't recall being late. Please delete this negative entry or send me a copy of the original notice of delinquency."

Third category. Those who fall under the third category with an account closed but a volume buyer would have to do something different from those in the first and second categories. Your strategy would depend on how long it has been since the account was closed. If it has been four years or fewer since your account was closed, you need to reestablish a customer relationship with the merchant. However, if your account has been on a merchant's database for at least five years, probably your account has been purged or is about to be purged. The best strategy is to request proof of delinquency, and because the account is purged, the merchant will not provide any and will end up deleting the negative entry.

In re-establishing a business relationship when it has been four years or fewer since your account was closed, you will ask the merchant to reopen your account if possible, or open a new account. For two or three months, concentrate all your purchases on this merchant and pay cash. Let me repeat, do not over spend your budget because you want to increase your credit score. Instead of paying someone else, you could channel all your buying power to this merchant who is going to help you. After the two or three months, make copies of all your cash receipts and enclose a letter to the merchant.

Let the merchant know you have been a customer with buying power, and despite the fact that your account was closed, you still love to shop at the store.

Also, disclose that recent cash receipts are enclosed for merchant's review. Request a one-time customer courtesy to reopen an account and correct negative entry with credit bureaus, and, in return, you will pay the delinquent amount in full. Don't forget to send a thank-you note to the merchant, after your account is reopened. Whatever you do, make sure you receive a letter from the merchant says that the account will be deleted or corrected to "paying as agreed" or "paid as agreed." This letter must be in your credit binder.

Your letter should be directed to the vice president of customer services. Because your account was previously closed, you will want the top person in the organization to know a previous customer with buying power could be lost if your demands are not met. Be sure the vice president's office is at the address on the letter. You may have to call to find out the name and address before mailing your letter.

If your account has been closed five years or more, re-establishing a business relationship may not be the best way to go but it is worth a try. Your account may have been purged from the merchant's database. Your letter may include a paragraph that asks the company to tell you if your account number cannot be located. Be sure you have the correct account number; read it back to yourself to make sure the numbers are correct. The last thing you need is a cat-and-mouse game because you have the wrong account number. They will write you way before the 30-day period, saying that you don't have the right account—just to waste your time.

One of your paragraphs should be a thank you for the way the customer service representatives have always handled your calls in a friendly and professional manner. An essential part of your letter is your request to delete or send you proof that your account was ever delinquent. "You are reporting to the credit bureau that I was delinquent on my account. I always pay bills on time. Please delete this negative entry or send me a copy of the original notice of delinquency."

Fourth category. The last category is a customer whose account was closed, who was never a volume buyer and who was never on time with payments. If you are classified in this category, you may find it a little difficult to deal with a merchant. If the business cannot find a good reason to help you, they will not and all you get is a letter, saying that you did not pay your bill on time. And their reply will say something such as, "We will not change accurate information on your credit report."

If you are in this situation, you must first check when was the first time this late payment was reported to the credit bureau. If you have one to six months before the negative entry must come off your credit report, you should wait it out. If you cannot wait, then you should request proof of information.

Your letter should be addressed to the manager of the company. You must make sure the name of the manager is on the letter and on the envelope. Also, be sure the manager's office is at the address where you are sending your letter. You may have to call to confirm the address.

Customers who fall in this category should send their letters by certified mail without return receipt requested. For proof of delivery, staple your certified receipt and the signed returned receipt on a copy of the letter in your file. The tone of your letter should be friendly. Try to avoid using legal language or the fact that you know you're right. Do not use a threatening tone like you will send the merchant to court if they don't reply to you immediately. All letters for proof of information should be friendly and professional. The only purpose of your writing is to request proof that you were late, and your letter should say something such as, "You are reporting to the credit bureau that I was delinquent on my account. I have always paid my bills on time and cannot recall being late. Please delete this negative entry or send me a copy of the original notice of delinquency."

Letter to Merchant for Proof of Information

There are three steps to removing negative entries on your credit report when dealing with merchants.

1.   First, request to delete or provide proof of information with a follow-up letter after 30 days.
2.   Second, ask the credit bureau to delete for lack of proof of information.

3.   Third, ask the government to force the credit bureau to obey the law, since you did not receive proof that the account is yours within the time allowed by law.

If you discover a negative entry in your credit report from a merchant when you were spreading your credit report, it is time to communicate directly with the merchant. Negative entries from merchants are mostly located in the middle of the report, with few in the public and collection sections. Merchants are always willing to help, unlike the collection agencies.

This is when you are going to appreciate the value of having the names, addresses, and phone numbers of all subscribers on your credit report. You may have to test the phone number by calling the merchant and confirming the address you received from the credit bureau. If the phone number is disconnected and there is no forwarding number, it is a strong indication the merchant's business is closed or has relocated. Dial the number three times to make sure you are dialing the right number you received from the credit bureau.

Write a letter to the merchant with ONLY the address from the credit bureau, and send your letter using the following instructions:

1.   Address your letter to the manager of customer services.
2.   Disclose that the merchant is reporting a delinquent account or whatever the negative entry is that's on your credit report.
3.   Disclose that you have never been delinquent and the merchant should delete the negative information from your credit report.
4.   List your account number.
5.   If the merchant does not delete, ask them to provide proof of information, including proof of signature, agreement, invoices, statements, and notices of delinquency. This is the most important statement in this letter.
6.   Send your letter certified mail with return receipt requested and type the certified mail number on your letter.

Sample Letter for Proof of Information

John Doe
1234 Adam St.
Dallas, TX 75111

January 1, 2004

Manager Customer Service
ABC Corporation
4321 Adam Lane
Atlanta, GA 30374
Certified Mail #1234 5678 9123 4567 8912
Return Receipt Requested

Dear Manager:

You are reporting to the credit bureau that I was delinquent on account number 999999911111222. I was never delinquent.

Please delete this negative entry from my credit report, or provide me with proof of information, including agreements, invoices, statements with signatures, and notices of delinquencies as evidence of obligor's indebtedness.

As required by law, "such amount (can)not be reported as delinquent to any third party until the creditor has met the requirements."

Your earliest reply is greatly appreciated.

Sincerely,

John Doe

What Reply to Expect from the Merchant

You should be expecting the reply to your first letter within 30 days. Most merchants will reply immediately after investigating your account. However, some merchants will drag their feet till the end of the 30-day period allowed by law. If you add the following statement to your letter to the merchant, "Please reply by certified mail, return receipt requested," it will force the merchant to make sure the letter gets to you and to keep proof of delivery for evidence. If you do not receive the reply, you can use your instruction as a defense. Action or inaction from the merchant will fall into four categories:

- Return to sender
- Merchant did not reply
- Merchant replied and wants more information
- Merchant replied and promised to delete negative entry
- Merchant replied and enclosed some or none of the information requested
- Merchant replied and enclosed all the information requested

1.   **Return to sender.** If the business has closed, the mail delivery service will return your letter undelivered. Another reason your letter would be returned to you undelivered is an incorrect address.

You would not receive a return-to-sender letter because the business is closed if you still have an open account with the merchant; after all, you have been sending your payments to the merchant. Between you and the customer department, somebody had the address wrong. The first thing you should do when you receive a return-to-sender reply is check the address on the envelope with the address on your credit report or the source of the information. If you receive the address by calling the customer service department, it is advisable to call back and ask for the same address, and repeat it back to the representative. Watch for error of omission (i.e., writing 780 instead of 7800) or error of transposition (i.e., writing 2565 instead of 2656).

If everything checks out all right and there are no errors, send a final letter to the vice president of the company. Enclose your first letter and ask that the reply be sent to you by certified mail with return receipt requested.

2.   **Merchant did not reply**. Since you are writing with the address from the credit bureau, one of the reasons the merchant received your letter and did not reply is that the merchant does not have proof of information. If your account is closed, it may have been purged from the system.

After 30 days, write a second letter to the vice president of customer service. You must enclose a copy of your previous letter, and your letter should reference the date of your last letter, not the date on the certified mail receipt. You must write the date you are expecting a reply from the merchant on your Communication Tracking System.

Your letter should be friendly reminding the merchant that it has been more than 30 days since you wrote the company. Before you send your second letter. Double check the name and address to make sure it matches with the name and address from the credit bureau.

3.   **Merchant replied and wants more information.** Many times when the information in your letter is incorrect or incomplete to pull your account, the merchant will ask for more information. To make sure you do not get this kind of letter, make sure the correct name on the account, the correct account number, and the correct address are listed in your first letter. Any of these simple mistakes could cost 30-60 days in credit repair process. If you receive this kind of letter, double check the name, address, and account number on your account bill and make sure it matches the information on the copy of the letter you sent to the merchant.

If you sent your previous letter to the manager of the company, most likely your letter was assigned to a representative who would investigate your case and reply. You must reply to whomever is referred to in the letter, because this person now has your file and would be working with you. Just remember that if this person is not cooperative, your next letter must be sent to top management—the vice president or the manager who referred you to that representative. In requesting more information from you, the merchant will identify exactly what information is needed and make sure you supply that specific information. Make it brief and send it back by certified mail, return receipt requested.

4.   **Merchant replied and promised to delete negative entry.** After reviewing your account, the merchant may have found out you are a volume buyer, and, nine times out of 10, will delete the negative entry on your credit report. The only person who can correct or delete a negative remark on your credit report is the originator, or in this case, the merchant.

Once you receive the good news, you must keep this letter in your credit binder and wait for 30 days to see if the changes are made. Next time you receive an updated copy of your credit report, check that the corrections were made by the merchant, as promised.

5.   **Merchant replied and enclosed some or none of the information requested.** A letter that encloses some of the information and not all of your requests is very suspicious. Therefore, receiving some information is as bad as not receiving anything at all. Most of the time, the information that was left out is exactly what you're looking for—the date, the amount, or other important information. Other times, the proof was not enclosed because the merchant does not have access to it— information may have been purged from the system and cannot be found.

You should reply directly to the vice president of customer services, not the manager. You want to include the fact that it is a requirement for the merchant to send information to a customer upon request. Tell the vice president what specific information you want and that without it, you cannot verify that the account belongs to you or is delinquent.

6.   **Merchant replied and enclosed all the information requested.** If the merchant encloses all the requested information, you have to verify the account to make sure it's yours. Examine all records and, if the

merchant proved the account is yours, look for the date of delinquency and calculate the cut-off date and waiting date to determine if you want to wait it out. Proceed to ask for a one-time courtesy, if the account is still open. If you do not get a one-time courtesy, proceed to decide on a one-time full payment or scheduled monthly payments with a promise to delete the negative entry.

After reviewing what happened with the previous scenarios, you will now write a follow-up letter to the merchant. Apply the following instructions to your letter:

- a. Address your letter to the vice president of customer services or a representative that has been assigned to your case.
- b. Acknowledge the receipt of the last letter without proof of information, as requested.
- c. You want the negative entry deleted or proof of information sent to you.
- d. The law requires the merchant, upon your request, to provide copies of documented evidence of obligor's indebtedness.
- e. List the proof of signature, proof of delinquency, and other proofs.
- f. Include the fact that the negative entries are costing you thousands of dollars due to a low credit score.
- g. Send your letter certified mail, return receipt requested and type the certified mail number on your letter.

Sample Follow-up Letter for Proof of Information

John Doe
1234 Adam St.
Dallas, TX 75111

January 1, 2004

Vice President, Customer Services
ABC Corporation
4321 Adam Lane
Atlanta, GA 30374
Certified Mail #1234 5678 9123 4567 8912
Return Receipt Requested

Dear Vice President:

I received your letter dated January 1, 2000; however, you did not enclose the proof of information as requested in my letter. The account #11122225555 you're reporting to the credit bureau does not belong to me.

Please delete this entry or, as required by law, I am formally requesting you to provide copies of documented evidence of obligor's indebtedness in the form of the following:

1.   Copies of signature
2.   Copies of agreement
3.   Copies of invoices
4.   Copies of statements
5.   Copies of notices of delinquencies

As required by law, "such amount (can)not be reported as delinquent to any third party until the creditor has met the requirements."

Your earliest reply is greatly appreciated.

Sincerely,
John Doe

Asking the Credit Reporting Agency to Delete for Lack of Proof

After you have written your first letter and a follow-up letter with the correct address, according to the law, if you do not receive proof of information that the account is yours, it's time to write the credit bureau to delete the negative entry or provide you with documented evidence of obligor's indebtedness.

The purpose of your letter to the credit bureau is for them to "Delete or provide proof of information, including proof of signature, agreement, invoices, bills, statements, and notices of delinquencies." It's good you have done your own investigation. What if you write to the credit bureau to delete without doing your own investigation and the credit bureau deletes? Two years down the road, the credit bureau could decide to reinsert the entry on your credit report. Because you knew it was deleted for lack of proof, you could challenge the reinsertion, which is against the law, unless the proof was supplied to you at the time of reinsertion.

There is no follow-up letter to the credit bureau when you are reporting the merchant did not provide you with proof of information. However, you must wait 45 days before taking the next step. You letter to the credit bureau should include the following:

1. Write to the manager of customer services, and include your account number.

2. Enclose a copy of the letter you sent to the merchant, with the comment that your request was not satisfied.

3. In a case of delinquency, you want the delinquency deleted because there is no proof you have had any delinquencies.

4. You want the credit bureau to delete, because the merchant failed to verify the account by providing documented evidence of obligor's indebtedness, as required by law.

5.   The negative entry is costing you thousands of dollars each year because of a low credit score. Send your letter certified mail, return receipt requested and type the certified mail number on the letter.

Sample Letter to Delete for Lack of Proof

John Doe
1234 Adam St.
Dallas, TX 75111

January 1, 2004

President, Customer Services
Equifax
P.O. Box 740241
Atlanta, GA 30374
Certified Mail #1234 5678 9123 4567 8912
Return Receipt Requested

Dear Manager:

My credit report bearing number 5555444441111 contains an account from ABC Corporation with account number 222224444333. Please delete this entry because the account does not belong to me or provide copies of the agreement, invoices, statements, a signature, and notices of delinquency.

ABC Corporation has failed to verify the account after my formal request of documented evidence of obligor's indebtedness, as required by law, per the enclosed letter.

In accordance with the Fair Credit Reporting Act, a person shall not furnish information relating to a consumer to any consumer reporting agency if the person has been notified by the consumer that specific information is inaccurate and the information is, in fact, inaccurate. The negative entry is costing me thousands of dollars a year.

Your earliest reply is greatly appreciated.

Sincerely,

John Doe

Letter to the Federal Trade Commission for Compliance

If after 45 days and no reply from the credit bureau or if you receive a reply that the negative account was not deleted, write the government and the BBB.

In this letter, you will report the credit bureau to the government, and you do not need a follow-up letter. The FTC, the Attorney General, and the BBB will normally reply to your letter.

Disclose the fact that you wrote to the merchant twice, without favorable response. Enclose your previous letters to the merchant. Disclose that the credit bureau refuses to make a thorough investigation into the matter; otherwise, the credit bureau would have provided you with the requested documented evidence of obligor's indebtedness.

You are now asking the government to force the credit bureau to delete the entry from your credit report or comply with the law by providing proof of information, including an agreement, invoices, statements, a signature and notices of delinquency.

Sample Letter for Compliance

John Doe
1234 Adam St.
Dallas, TX 75111

January 1, 2004

Federal Trade Commission
600 Pennsylvania Ave., N.W.
Washington, DC 20580
Certified Mail #1234 5678 9123 4567 8912
Return Receipt Requested

Dear Commissioner:

        Credit Report Lacks Proof of Account

I am filing a formal complaint against (XYZ Credit Bureau). I have requested the credit bureau to delete a negative entry on my credit report because of the following:

1.   The merchant fails to verify the account.
2.   The merchant fails to provide documented evidence of obligor's indebtedness.
3.   No one should report inaccurate information to the credit bureau.

It has been more than 45 days since the credit bureau refused to delete the entry or provide evidence that the account is mine from the merchant in the form of copies of the agreement, invoices, statements, a signature and notices of delinquency. I am enclosing my previous letters to the merchant and the credit bureau for your review and action. My Social Security number is 123-45-6789 and my telephone number is (123) 456-7890. Please open an investigation into this matter.

Your earliest reply is greatly appreciated.

Sincerely,
John Doe

Letter to the Attorney General and Better Business Bureau for Compliance

Write a similar letter to the Attorney General of your state and the BBB of your city, referring to the previous FTC letter. You may send your mail by certified mail only, and print details of delivery from the Internet.

Negotiation Strategies for Merchants

When you have received all the documents, decide how to pay the merchant. Before you approach the merchant, do your homework. Preparation is the key to success when it comes to negotiating with a merchant. As discussed earlier, you should first ask for a one-time courtesy, and when all else fails, arrange for payment, especially if it is a small amount of money. The objective of negotiation is to start making payments and, in return, the merchant will change a negative entry on your credit report to "paid as agreed."

At this point, you'll need to talk to the customer services manager through the representative who has been replying to your letters. You will need to call your contact person. Tell the representative you need to speak with the manager. If the manager was writing to you, speak to his or her supervisor. If the representative is hesitant about giving you the name of the person above him or her, say you are looking for the person who has the authority to make corrections on your account.

When you are on the phone, get the answers to some of the questions below. For most of these questions, you may already have the answers from your credit report, previous merchant's letters, and documents in your credit binder and just want to verify their accuracy.

- What was the date of delinquency?
- How much was the unpaid balance?
- Was this a late payment on an open account?
- Was this a late payment on a closed account?
- Has this account been sold to a third party?

- Has this account been assigned to a collection agency?
- Has this account been purged from the database?

a. **What was the date of delinquency?** You can test how honest the representative is by asking some questions for which you already have answers. When the date of delinquency confirms what you already know, immediately add seven years to that date and subtract one year from the result—this is the waiting date. If the waiting date falls before today's date, you are in the driver's seat. Write an action note, "Wait; will drop off," on the entry and quickly terminate the conversation. If waiting date comes after today's date, go to the next step.

b. **How much was the unpaid balance?** In negotiating with a merchant, the two most important words are time and money. How much is involved is very important to the merchant. The reason why the merchant refused to remove the negative entry on your credit report is money. If the amount is less than $400, it should be paid off in one payment or two payments. But if the amount is more than $500 and you can't pay it all at one time, negotiate scheduled payments with a discount.

c. **Was this a late payment on an open account?** If your account is still open with a late payment, and if the waiting date falls after today's date, ask for a one-time courtesy with a promise to not be late again. If the representative gives you a one-time courtesy, you need him or her to send you a note to document the agreement. If you do not get a one-time courtesy, begin the process of paying off and closing the business relationship with this merchant.

d. **Was this a late payment on a closed account?** If your account is already closed, there is not much you can do. There are a few ways to handle a closed account. The first one is to pay the amount, if it's very small ($400 or less) or whatever your cash flow allows. The second way is to wait because a merchant is not ready to waste his or her time on an account that is already closed.

e. **Has this account been sold to a third party?** What if your account was sold to another company? Ask for the name, address, and phone number of that company. The new company may have initiated a collection process by first reporting to the credit bureau. If you look carefully you can see the name of the new company listed on your credit report. Calculate both the cut-off date and the waiting date. If the account is too old, let it expire and come off by itself from your credit report.

f. **Has this account been sent to a collection agency?** If your account has been assigned but not sold to a collection agency, you can still negotiate with the merchant. Most collection contracts allow merchants to collect from customers. It would be easier to deal with the merchant than the collection agency. You must be able to offer more than the collection agency would return to the merchant for the deal to go through. The merchant could accept any offer close to 60% of the original amount. Don't use words like percent, discount, or phrases such as 30 cents on a dollar.

When you are negotiating with the merchant, offer to pay one half of the amounts and do not use the words half, percentage or 50 cents on a dollar. For example, if you owe $500, say, "I'm sending you a check for $345 right away so we can close this case." If you are still a customer, add the fact that you want to continue to be a loyal customer.

g. **Has this account been purged from the database?** To create more space in the system, some companies have a policy of purging or cleaning out old accounts from the database. An account is considered old five years after it has been closed or was delinquent.

The reason you were told, in the reply, that the negative entry would not be changed on your credit report might be that the account has been purged and cannot be found. While you are on the phone, it will not take long before the manager will tell you that the account has been purged, that is after you started asking pertinent questions about the account, such as the account balance and the date of delinquency. Your last statement should be "Could you please send me a letter that the account is purged?" Find out the approximate date it would take for the letter to reach you. Ask the manager what date to call back if you don't receive the letter. If you don't receive any reply after that date, don't call, but write a letter. Thank him or her for speaking with you on a certain date and write that you want to confirm the discussion that your account could not be found for payment because it has been purged from the system.

If you agree on a full or scheduled payment, you should send a letter to the merchant for signature. You may use the following instructions and facts in writing your letter:

1. Send your letter to the representative you made the agreement with over the phone. Refer to the date of your discussion.

2. State the amount you agreed on for full or scheduled payments.

3. State the fact that the representative agreed to change the negative entry to "paid as agreed" after you made the first payment. Enclose a stamped, self-addressed envelope.

4. After you receive the signed agreement letter, send a check or money order with a copy of the agreement as certified mail, return receipt requested. For scheduled payments, send the last payment with a copy of the agreement.

5. For a one-time, full payment, write on the back of the check or money order, "Full payment, promised to change entry to pay as agreed" Make photocopy of check or money order, front and back, for your record.

6. Request your credit report to make sure the entry is changed to "pay as agreed."

7. Send your letter certified mail, return receipt requested and type the certified mail number on the letter.

Negotiating a One-Time Payment

Time and money is everything when it comes to negotiating. In an earlier chapter, we talked about calculating the cut-off date and the waiting date, now it's time to really apply those principles, specifically when the merchant supplies all the necessary documents that prove you are the owner of the account or that it is actually delinquent.

A one-time, full payment is good for small amounts like $400 or less or any amount of money your cash flow can handle. Most negotiations should be done over the phone. As discussed in the previous section, talk to someone who can make a decision for the company without being fired or reprimanded. Bear in mind that only a manager can make such a decision.

Before you make an offer to pay off the entire amount, ask for a discount. If the date of delinquency falls before the cut-off date, and you really want to pay off the debt, negotiate for 50% of the original amount. Before you make an offer, ask what is the date of delinquency, and say that you want to pay off this account despite the fact that the expiration date with the credit bureau is coming soon. Start below 50% of the amount owed, and finally go a little over 50%, but do not use the word "percentage" over the phone.

If today's date falls after the cut-off and waiting dates, most likely, the merchant would accept offers between 60% and 70%. For a debt that is less than $400, most merchants want full payment and for anything more than $500, the merchant would be open to negotiating a discount.

Do not use round numbers like $200 or $500. Always use odd-sounding numbers that would not equate to an even percentage when the merchant does the calculating. Use numbers like $395 or $537 in your negotiating.

After you have agreed to an amount, get it in writing. The best way to do that is to ask the merchant to do the writing. Say something such as, "Please send me a letter or a note on our agreement, and write that I promised to send you a check as soon as I received the letter." Find out what date to expect the agreement. Restate or summarize your agreement, by saying, "I promise to pay the sum of $395 as soon as I receive the letter and you promise to delete the negative entry from the credit bureau."

At this point, say something such as, "If it's a problem for you, I can write the letter and send it to you for signature." Nine times out 10, the merchant will pass on the job to you. It is your duty now to copy the letter below, modify it to fit your situation and mail it to the merchant for signature. You don't want to make the payment and still have the negative entry on your credit report. The signed letter from the merchant is evidence of your agreement.

Sample Letter for a One-Time, Full Payment

John Doe
1234 Adam St.
Dallas, TX 75111

Vice President, Customer Services
ABC Corporation
4321 Adam Lane
Atlanta, GA 30374
Certified Mail #1234 5678 9123 4567 8912
Return Receipt Requested

Dear Vice President:

I appreciate your time in discussing my account number 555544443333. Per our discussion on January 1, 2000, I agreed to pay ABC Corporation $47 as a full and final payment on the account.

In return, within five business days of receiving final payment, you agreed to change the negative entry associated with this account on my credit report to "paid as agreed." I will send $47 as soon as this letter of agreement is signed and returned to me in the enclosed stamped and self-addressed envelope.

Your earliest reply is greatly appreciated.

Sincerely,

John Doe

                                        Agreed and accepted
                                        By_____
                                        Name_____
                                        Date_____

Negotiating Scheduled Payments

Negotiating for scheduled payment is much like negotiating for the full payment. The major difference is that the merchant will change the negative entry on your credit report to "paid as agreed" after you make the first payment.

By now, you know what numbers to use and what percentages of the balance to offer based on the cut-off date. Remember that any amount less than $400 is not good for scheduled payments, but it is good for a big discount with a one-time payment promise. However, it would not hurt to ask to split the $400 into four monthly payments. Amounts of more than $500 can be split into five to 10 payments; balances of $1,000 or more should be negotiated for a 10-month payment plan but not more than a year to make the last payment.

A better way to negotiate for a scheduled payment that's acceptable to a merchant is to pay half of the balance now and split the remaining balance into 12 months.

You should get the merchant to allow you to write the letter for his or her signature as previously discussed. When you start restating or summarizing your agreement, most merchants will want you to do the writing. No letter is acceptable to you if it does not say the merchant will change the negative account on your credit report to "paid as agreed." You do not want to delete your account with a merchant, thereby losing many months or years of credit history.

Sample Letter for Scheduled Payments

John Doe
1234 Adam St.
Dallas, TX 75111

January 1, 2004

President
ABC Corporation
4321 Adam Lane
Atlanta, GA 30374
Certified Mail #1234 5678 9123 4567 8912
Return Receipt Requested

Dear President:

I appreciate your time in discussing my account. This is a summary of our January 1, 2000 discussion. I agreed to pay ABC Corporation $147 every month for 12 months starting January 2000 and ending December 2000 as a full and final payment on account number 55555444411112222.

If, for any reason, payment does not reach your office in any month, the past due amount will be cured in the following months, as long as the entire amount is paid in full before December 31, 2000.

In return, within five business days of receiving the first payment, you agreed to change the negative entry associated with this account on my credit report to "paid as agreed." I will send $147 as soon as this letter of agreement is signed and returned to me in the enclosed stamped self-addressed envelope.

Your earliest reply is greatly appreciated.

Sincerely,

John Doe   Agreed and accepted
                                  By_____
                                  Name_____
                                  Date_____

Asking Merchant to Delete Inquiries

After reviewing your credit report, you may find out you have too many inquiries on it. Four inquires or more in one year are too many and should be reduced. Your first step is to calculate the cut-off date using the legal two years to see if these inquiries are about to drop from your credit report. If you cannot wait, find the inquiries you did not initiate. Write to those merchants and demand that they delete inquiries since you did not initiate any solicitation for credit nor had you any business relationship with them.

The best way to stop harassment from the marketing companies and block the credit bureaus from selling your credit information is to opt out of their marketing database. If you are tired of getting junk mail, opting out stops companies from sniffing through your credit report in the name of legitimate business needs. File your intent to opt out with all three major credit bureaus in a certified letter, return receipt requested.

Be sure to file a copy of your opt-out letter in your credit report binder, and wait for violators who might be listed on your credit report. You know what to do when a company slips and tells you the information about you was provided by the credit bureaus, after you have filed your opt-out request.

Sample Letter to Delete Inquiries

John Doe
1234 Adam St.
Dallas, TX 75111

January 1, 2004

Vice President
ABC Corporation
4321 Adam Lane
Atlanta, GA 30374
Certified Mail #1234 5678 9123 4567 8912
Return Receipt Requested

Dear Vice President:

I was reviewing my credit report and noticed that you made an illegal inquiry on me. I want you to delete this inquiry immediately from my credit report with the credit bureaus or provide me the following proof of information:

1.   Copies of application
2.   Copies of signature
3.   Copies of agreement

As required by law, any person who knowingly and willfully obtains information on a consumer from a consumer reporting agency, under false pretenses, shall be fined under Title 18 (Crimes and Criminal Procedure), imprisoned for no more than 2 years, or both.

Your inquiry has reduced my credit score and is costing me money. If I do not hear from you in 30 days, I will file a formal complaint with the FTC.

Your earliest reply is greatly appreciated.

Sincerely,
John Doe

Asking Merchant to Confirm Account History

After you have completed the list of positives page in your communication tracking system, you may notice that there is an account that is being reported by one credit bureau and not the others. Review the account and confirm the following characteristics before adding it to your credit report:

- Account was with a reputable company not a cash loan finance company
- Account had more than a nine month history
- Account was never late
- Account had positive status with at least one credit bureau.

Before you write the credit bureau to add the account, call the merchant you opened the account with and ask if the merchant reports to all three major credit bureaus. If the answer is yes, then you should request that the merchant report your credit to the omitted credit bureau. If the answer is no, have the representative tell you the account history status as listed previously in the "confirm account history" letter. Tell the representative that you are sending a letter to confirm your discussion. Write a letter to the merchant and when you receive your reply, confirm the four positive account characteristics as listed below. If everything checks out, use the following steps to add a positive account to your credit report:

1.   Complete the list of positive accounts and find which credit bureau is not reporting your positive entry.

2.   Check your credit report to make sure that the one credit bureau is reporting the account with a positive status.

3.   Call to find out if the merchant reports to all credit bureaus; if yes, request that the merchant add your positive entry.

4.   Complete your oral communication page in the communication tracking system with the date, time you called, name of whom you spoke to, and when the addition is to take place.

5.   If a merchant does not report a particular credit bureau write a letter to the merchant to confirm account history, and then write to the credit bureau to add your positive account.

6.   Include your Social Security number and your date of birth on the letter to the credit bureau.

7.   Ask for an updated copy of your credit report.

8.   Send your letter certified mail, return receipt requested and type the certified mail number on the letter.

Sample Letter to Confirm Account History

John Doe
1234 Adam St.
Dallas, TX 75111

January 1, 2004

(The name of the representative who you spoke with)
ABC Corporation
4321 Adam Lane
Atlanta, GA 30374
Certified Mail #1234 5678 9123 4567 8912
Return Receipt Requested

Dear (name of representative who you spoke with):

Please confirm the following account history as was provided to me during our January 1, 2000 conversation by signing and returning the enclosed letter.

1.   Name of merchant = ABC Corporation
2.   Name of customer = John Doe
3.   Account number = 123456789
4.   Credit limit = $2,000
5.   Monthly payment = $95.25
6.   Current balance = $0.00
7.   Account status = satisfactory, never late
8.   Date open = 1/1/2000

Your earliest reply is greatly appreciated.

Sincerely,
John Doe

                                   Verified and confirmed
                                   By_____
                                   Name_____
                                   Date_____

Sample Letter to Add Positive Account

John Doe
1234 Adam St.
Dallas, TX 75111

January 1, 2004

Manager, Customer Services
Equifax
P.O. Box 740241
Atlanta, GA 30374
Certified Mail #1234 5678 9123 4567 8912

Dear Manager:

I have had an account with ABC Corporation for 24 months with satisfactory payment history, and would like the account to be added to my credit report.

Enclosed is a confirmation letter from ABC Corporation that shows the account was never late. If there is a fee for this service, please let me know by sending a bill.

My date of birth is January 1, 1900. Copies of my Social Security card and utility bill are enclosed for proof of identity.

Your earliest reply is greatly appreciated.

Sincerely,

John Doe

Chapter 9

Working with
Collection Agencies

Validating Debt and Collection Agency

Collection agents have gotten a lot of condemnation in recent years, far more than they deserve. There are lots of honest and law-abiding citizens in the collection business. From time to time, you will run into some unscrupulous agents, who want to gouge you out of your money by any means necessary. Just keep your eyes open at all times. You must understand that in the world of the collection business, money is everything.

If you do not pay your debt, in most cases after 120 days, your account will be turned over to a collection agency. The agency will start the process of validating your debt with you, the debtor, as required by law. The validation process is one of the most important steps in dealing with a collection agency. The same law that authorizes the collection agency to validate the debt and you, also, authorizes you to validate the debt, the collection agency, and the original creditor or merchant. According to the Fair Debt Collection Practices Act, a collection agent will contact you and within five days of the initial communication, they will send you a written notice of the following:

1.   The amount of the debt

2.   The name of the creditor to whom the debt is owed

3.   A statement that unless the consumer, within 30 days after receipt of notice, disputes the validity of the debt, the debt is assumed to be valid

4.   A statement that if the consumer notifies the debt collector, in writing, within 30 days that a portion of the debt is disputed, the debt collector will obtain verification of the debt or copy of judgment

5.   A statement that upon customer's written request within 30 days, the debt collector will provide the consumer with the name and address of the original creditor, if different from the current creditor.

The law also says that if the debtor, in writing, within 30 days requests the name and address of the original creditor, the collector should cease collection of the debt until the validation process is completed."

Most consumers would panic when they receive a collection agency's letter and probably put the letter away or toss it in the garbage because of fear. This is a grave mistake; rather, the consumer should start validating the debt, the collection agency, and the merchant. The purpose of validating the collection agency is to request the name and the address of the original creditor and to make sure the agent is currently representing the creditor. What if the collection agency is slow in collecting from the debtor and the creditor decided to cancel the contract and assign the account to another agency or decides to use an in-house representative to collect, you could be paying the wrong agency. In response to the collection agency's letter, you would be writing back within 30 days requesting the name, address, and phone number of the original creditor as required by law. Your letter should be certified mail, return receipt requested.

The validation process is very important, not only would you use it to find out what kind of collection agency you are dealing with, but also what kind of deal you can make directly with the merchant. If your account was assigned, but not sold, the merchant would be eager to make a deal with you right away.

Analyzing Debt and Collection Agency

After you receive the name, address, and phone number of the original creditor, contact the merchant by phone. If you don't have the phone number, send a letter to the merchant to verify the collection agency. The purpose of writing is to get the merchant's phone number and the name of a contact person. Now that you have the phone number, find out everything you can about the debt and the collection agency with which you are dealing.

Before you go to war, you must know the strengths and weaknesses of your enemy and for the purpose of analyzing collection agencies, you should know that there are two kinds of collection agents:

1.   Collection agents who work for a merchant on commission. In this case, the merchant assigns delinquent accounts to a collector and, in return, receives a percentage of the total debt collected. These are called commission agents.

2.   Collection agents who buy delinquent accounts from merchants at a
      discount without commission. At the end of every quarter or year, big
      businesses sell a block of their delinquent accounts to collection agents
      at a discount based on age and ability to collect the debt. These are
      called independent agents.

Most of the time, when the debt is less than $400, the agency will not even
write to you, especially if the agency has bigger accounts than yours to
collect—or should I say bigger fish to fry. You would have to look at your
credit report to begin the validation process of the debt, first, with the
collection agent and, second, with the original merchant.

If you are working with a collection agency, find out which category your
account falls under, and be able to design a strategy that fits that category.
When you correctly classify your debt by using these basic tests, the job is half
done. Following are the five basic categories or questions about your debt and
the collection agent:

- Is the cut-off date or waiting date favorable?
- How much is your delinquent account?
- Is this a commission agent?
- Is this an independent agent?
- Is the statute on your debt expired?

Is the cut-off date or waiting date favorable? This is, by far, the most
important question you will ask yourself during the analyzing process.
Collection agents are very aggressive and all they think about is getting the
check in the mail. Time is the greatest enemy to a collection agent. You must
immediately calculate the cut-off date. If the date is favorable, that is, if the
cut-off date falls before today's date, you must write the credit bureau to delete
the entry from your credit report. Also, check your credit report next time you
receive an updated credit report copy. If the cut-off date falls after today's
date, calculate the waiting date by subtracting one year from the cut-off date to
see if the waiting date will fall before today's date. This is the time you could
use to wait for the delinquent account to expire and drop from your report. It's
worth it to wait one year rather than dealing with a collection agent. If you
have a pressing need, you can use six months to calculate the waiting date.

Some collection agents are very rude over the phone. Agents will put the heat on you when you call. This is the reason they have their 1-800 number prominently displayed on your credit report. A good professional agent will write your cut-off date on the front cover of your file. The heat will be turned on high if you call around the cut-off date. The agent will classify you as an informed consumer if you say something about the cut-off date.

How much is your delinquent account? The amount you owe to a collection agent is very important. Monthly production is based on total amount collected; therefore, if you owe $1,000 or more, you are considered a big fish and the agent will try every trick to collect. But if your debt is $400 or less, agents will not want to waste their time on you when they could use the same time and energy chasing after $5,000-$10,000 accounts.

Is this a commission agent? In general, commission agents are not as aggressive as independent agents. However, commission agents are very aggressive when it comes to a high dollar account as explained previously. Merchants can also make deals directly with a customer if the collector is a commission agent.

If an agent is giving the merchant 60% of what is collected, the merchant might be willing to accept 50% from you now rather than wait for the collection agent to collect—if at all—on a future date. This will change your negative entry to "paid as agreed" to retain your years of credit history. With a collection agency, you want the account deleted because you don't want the name of a collection agency on your credit report.

Is this an independent agent? In general, independent agents are more aggressive than commission agents. Remember, independent agents are working for themselves, and therefore, will do anything to collect their money from you. The agent bought the account at a discount from the merchant with the hope of collecting full payment or at a little discount of only 10% -20% to you. In other words, an independent agent wants all the money—and wants it all now!

Is the statute on your debt expired? I'm a strong advocate of paying your debt even if it has dropped from your credit report, but get an agreement so that the debt will never be reinserted onto your credit report. However, you should stand up against a collection agent that harasses you and makes life miserable for you. When you default on a high-dollar debt, a merchant may file a suit against you for judgment. If you don't attend the trial, the merchant can get a judgment against you without your knowledge, but the judgment will be reported on the public information section of your credit report. However, if the merchant never takes you to court, in some states, after four years, the merchant or creditor can no longer take you to court, but report your account to the credit bureau—that's it!

When you call a lawyer for the initial free consultation, ask for your state's statute of limitations on your kind of debt, namely, oral debt, written debt, promissory note, closed-ended, and revolving or open-ended debts. That a debt appears on your credit report from a collection agency does not mean you should pay it if the statute of limitations has passed. If you determine that the merchant can no longer take you to court, this is a bargaining chip with the collection agency. Remind the collection agency that the statute of limitations on the debt has passed and that it will also drop off from your credit report after seven years from the date of delinquency. That would really get him or her to negotiate with you immediately.

Requesting Proof of Information

After you have completed the due diligence or validated the collection agency with the merchant and have done the debt and collection agency analysis as described previously, you are ready to deal with the collection. Your success is assured because you are loaded with important information about the debt and the collection agency. Your strategy in dealing with a collection agent with regard to proof of information depends on the cut-off date and the amount on your credit report. The following are four categories in which your late payment account and your relationship with the collection agent may be classified:

1.   Cut-off date is close,
       Amount owed is large

2.   Cut-off date is close,
        Amount owed is small

3.   Cut-off date is not close,
        Amount owed is large

4.   Cut-off date is not close,
        Amount owed is small

First category. If your account falls on the first category, in which the cut-off date is close and the amount you owe is large, you are in driver's seat, but proceed with caution. A good collection agency already knows the cut-off date is close and wants to make a deal fast. Let me repeat, I'm a strong advocate of paying off your delinquent accounts even when it drops from your credit report, ONLY to a merchant not a collection agent. You are taking a high moral ground when you pay your delinquent account that has already been deleted from your credit report. However, you must secure a written agreement ONLY from the merchant not a collection agent that the deleted account you are now paying off will never be reinserted into your credit report as "paid collection." Otherwise, you will have to wait another seven years for this negative entry to drop from your credit report. Never make this kind of deal with a collection agent.

Your first letter should be addressed to the manager and your reply may come from a representative who has been assigned to your account. A comment may already be in your file that the account is about to drop from the credit report and should be expedited with a discount for easy close.

If there is one place where you should send your letter by certified mail, return receipt requested, this is it. Sending your proof of information letter by ordinary mail may open a door to delays and misplacements. Include the fact that you are requesting your reply be sent by certified mail, return receipt requested. It does not matter if your request is honored or not. What's important is that the agency will never use loss of mail as an excuse. In your letter, request proof of information regarding the delinquent account. Specifically, request copies of proof of signature, agreements, invoices, statements, and notices of delinquency.

Your letter may start with the fact that they are reporting you to the credit bureaus but the negative entry is becoming outdated and obsolete. You could add, "I'd like to pay off this account if you can verify it belongs to me, and please note that very soon, the account will be outdated and obsolete with the credit bureaus." The purpose is to put the agency on notice that you know the account will soon be dropping from your credit report. Because the amount involved is high and the cut-off date is close, they will make you a good offer to get you to pay. To this end, you may add information like, "I do not think this account is mine, but I would like to know the lowest, I mean the very lowest amount the agency would accept to close the case." You are making an offer without admitting guilt or that the account is yours.

Second category. After you review your credit reports and other documents, you may classify yourself in the second category—the cut-off date is close and the amount is small. You have a better chance of dealing with any collection agency in your own terms when you fall under this category.

You should be addressing your letter to the manager not the president or the supervisor. Managers have caps on how much they can make a call on and not be reprimanded or fired. Any account of $1,000 or less should be directed to the manager. All accounts of $1,000 or more should be addressed to the president, especially if the cut-off date is close. He or she will decide right away how much your account should be discounted.

Send your letter by certified mail, return receipt requested, and request that the agency send your reply certified mail, return receipt requested. You would be asking for proof of signature, agreements, invoices, statements, and notices of delinquency.

You may begin your letter with the fact that you want to pay off the account if it is yours, despite the fact that the delinquent account is becoming outdated with the credit bureaus. An important part of your letter is to find out the lowest amount the collection agency is willing to accept to close your case.

Third category. If your account is classified in the third category, it means that your cut-off date is not close and the amount is large. This is not the best position to be in. Collection agencies are very aggressive is pursuing accounts of this nature. This is the reason why bad collection agents like to redate your account on your credit report, by changing the date of delinquency every year to make the account stay on your credit report—forever!

Your letter should be addressed to the president because the delinquent amount is large. Send your letter by certified mail, return receipt requested and ask for the same courtesy. You will be requesting proof of signature, agreements, invoices, statements, and notices of delinquency, because the account is not yours. Ask for the lowest amount the collection agency will accept for full payment without admitting guilt.

Fourth category. The fourth and final category is one in which the cut-off date is not close but the amount is small. This is a better position than the one previously mentioned in which the amount is large. Because the cut-off date is not close, you do not want a collection agency entry on your credit report. It is worth every effort to pay off the delinquent account and close the case. It is bad enough that a prospective merchant is seeing that you are delinquent for a puny $50, but it's even worse if that same $50 is knocking off 50 points from your credit score. If you want to pay off the account because the amount is small, have the collection sign an agreement that the entry will be deleted not changed to any other comment, even "paid as agreed," because you do not want the name of a collection agency on your credit report. Let me repeat, the collection agency must sign an agreement only to delete the entry before you send a penny to them.

You should be writing to the manager, since the amount is small, and send your letter by certified mail, return receipt requested. Ask for copies of signature, agreements, invoices, statements, and notices of delinquency.

Letter to the Collection Agency for Proof of Information

By now, you should understand the steps to removing a negative entry from your credit report. First, request that the collection agencies delete or provide proof of information, with a follow-up letter if the reply is not received in 30 days. Second, ask the credit bureau to delete for lack of proof of information.

Third, ask to the government authorities to force the credit bureau to obey the law.

You should have the address and phone number of the collection agency from the credit bureau. Now, you are ready to deal with the collection agency. You may want to call the number of the collection agency to confirm the address. If the address from the credit bureau is wrong, you will receive a return-to-sender reply. Keep it as proof, should the credit bureau claim they used the same address to reach the collection agency. Your letter should include the following instructions and facts:

1.   Write to the manager of customer services. The collection agency is listing account number 44445555888 with the credit bureau. The account is not yours.

2.   Request that the account be deleted or that they forward documented proof of obligor's indebtedness in the form of proof of signature, agreements, invoices, statements, and notices of delinquency.

3.   List the documented evidence you need, and send your letter certified mail, return receipt requested and type the certified mail number on the letter.

Sample Letter for Proof of Information

John Doe
1234 Adam St.
Dallas, TX 75111

January 1, 2004

Manager, Customer Services
XYZ Collection Agency
4321 Adam Lane
Atlanta, GA 30374
Certified Mail #1234 5678 9123 4567 8912
Return Receipt Requested

Dear Manager:

You are reporting to the credit bureau that I was delinquent on account number 999999111111222. I was never delinquent.

Please delete the entry from the credit bureau or provide me the following verification of debt:

1.   Copies of signature
2.   Copies of agreements
3.   Copies of invoices
4.   Copies of statements
5.   Copies of notices of delinquencies

As required by law, I am formally requesting the name and address of the original creditor and demanding that you cease collection of debt until verification of debt be completed. As required by law, such amount cannot be reported as delinquent to any third party until the creditor has met the requirements.

Your earliest reply is greatly appreciated.

Sincerely,

John Doe

What Reply to Expect from a Collection Agency

After you've sent your first letter for proof of information, within 30 days you should be expecting your reply. If you have sent your letter as recommended previously, you will be certain of the kind of reply you will be getting or not getting.

The only thing standing between you and a collection agent is money. Producing copies of signature, agreements, invoices, and statements will surely prove that you are dealing with the legitimate collection agency.

If your delinquent account is more than $500, the reply to your first letter might be accompanied with an offer for settlement of debt, if you are dealing with a commission agency. There will be no need for a second request for proof of information, and communication with collectors will speed up into negotiation.

The following are six different types of letters you may receive from a collection agent and these replies will depend on the nature of your first request for information:

- Return to sender
- Agency did not reply
- Agency replied and wants more information
- Agency replied and promised to delete negative entry
- Agency replied and enclosed all the information with an offer
- Agency replied and enclosed some or no information with an offer

1.   **Return to sender.** If the collection agency happened to go out of business or relocate to another part of the city without a forwarding address, your letter will be returned to you. When you receive a return-to-sender letter, the first thing you'll do is double check the address on the envelope to confirm that it is correct. Have someone do this for you; two heads are better than one. Write a follow-up letter to the vice president of the agency. If you confirmed the address you used is correct, ask the credit bureau to delete the entry because you cannot locate the collection agency. The credit bureaus cannot say they need to

contact the collection agency, since the incorrect address came from them.

2. **Agency did not reply.** If you do not get a reply after 30-45 days, you double check the address on the certified receipt to make sure you wrote to the correct agency. After the verification, contact the credit bureau because the collection agency did not verify debt as required by law.

3. **Agency replied and wants more information.** If the agency wants more information, they will have to tell you exactly what information they are seeking. Send that information and nothing more. At this time, the collection agency may be buying time to investigate your account. Give them another 15 days, making it a total of 45 days, to reply to the letter in full.

4. **Agency replied and promised to delete negative entry.** The agency may promise to delete the entry because the account does not belong to you. Keep this letter in your credit file to send to the credit bureau in case the collection agency does not delete.

    You will rarely get this kind of letter, unless they find another person to whom the account belongs. Even if they know the account is not yours, collection agents do not have the time to write to you that the account is not yours—they just ignore you!

5. **Agency replied and enclosed all the information with an offer.** If the agency enclosed all the information requested, examine all records carefully, especially the signature and the date to make sure the account is actually yours. Now decide if you want to deal with the collection agency or wait. If you have a pressing need such as an impending purchase, negotiate for a one-time payment or scheduled monthly payments.

    If the agency sent you all the information, they are certain that the account belongs to you. So your two options are to pay it all now or schedule monthly payments, or wait, especially if the cut-off or waiting date is close.

6.   **Agency replied and enclosed some or no information with an offer.**
The agency is hiding something by not sending one of the documents
you're looking for. The speed in which you will receive this kind of
letter will depend on the delinquent amount, the cut-off date, and the
availability of the information. A good collection agent will have the
necessary proof of information already on file for high-dollar accounts.

If the cut-off date is close and the amount is more than $500, the
agency's offer may be around 70%, which is $350. Your second request
for information should be a counter offer of 50% in the form of an odd-
number amount. For example, if you owe $500, your offer should be
$259. Never use a round number in negotiation to avoid showing you
are working on percentage.

In your letter, do not say anything about the cut-off date or that you are
in a hurry to close this case—they already know that. Do not say
"Please reply at your earliest convenience." Tell the agency the account
is not yours, but you would like to close this case for $259—that way
you are not admitting guilt.

Now write a follow-up letter to the vice president of the company. The
purpose of your letter is to inform the collection agency that you need
all the proof of information requested to accurately confirm that the
account belongs to you. If after 30 days of your follow-up letter, you do
not receive a satisfactory reply, ask the credit bureaus to delete because
the agency did not verify as required by law. You may use the following
instructions and facts in your letter:

a.   Address your letter to the vice president.

b.   Acknowledge the receipt of the last letter without the proof of
information as requested.

c.   You want the negative entry deleted or proof of documentary
evidence of obligor's indebtedness sent to you.

   d. You need evidence in the form of proof of signature, agreements, invoices, statements, and notices of delinquency.

   e. Send your letter certified mail, return receipt requested and type the certified mail number on the letter.

Sample Follow-up Letter for Proof of Information

John Doe
1234 Adam St.
Dallas, TX 75111

January 1, 2004

Vice President
XYZ Collection Agency
4321 Adam Lane
Atlanta, GA 30374
Certified Mail #1234 5678 9123 4567 8912
Return Receipt Requested

Dear Vice President:

I received your letter dated January 1, 2004; however, you did not enclose the proof of information as requested in my letter. Please delete the entry from the credit bureau or provide verification of the debt, specifically copies of signature, agreements, invoices, statements, and notices of delinquencies.

The law requires, "If the consumer notifies the debt collector in writing that the debt or any portion thereof is disputed, the debt collector will obtain verification of the debt and a copy of such verification will be mailed to the consumer."

Also, as required by law, I am formally requesting the name and address of the original creditor and demanding that you cease collection of debt until verification of debt be completed; and "such amount not be reported as delinquent to any third party until the creditor has met the requirements."

Sincerely,

John Doe

Asking the Credit Reporting Agency
to Delete for Lack of Proof

Collection agencies don't really care about proof of information; they just want to be paid. After your follow-up request for proof of information, you should expect a different kind of reply.

You should wait at least 30 days after you have sent your follow-up letter to the vice president of the collection agency. If the collection agency does not have the proof, they will not even bother to reply your second letter. At this point, write to the credit bureau that you have written the collection agency and did not receive verification of debt as being yours.

Remember there are no follow-up letters to the credit bureau in this letter. You must wait for 45 days before taking the necessary action against the credit bureau. Your letter to the credit bureau should include the following instructions and facts:

1.   Write to the manager of customer services.

2.   You want the negative entry deleted because there is no proof the account is yours.

3.   In case of delinquency, you want the account to be deleted because there is no proof you have had any delinquent account.

4.   If the negative entry is not deleted, you need documented evidence of obligor's indebtedness in the following documentation: proof of signature, agreements, invoices, statements, and notices of delinquency.

5.   The negative entry is costing you thousands of dollars each year because of a low credit score.

6.   Enclose a copy of the previous letters to the collection agency.

7.   Send your letter certified mail, return receipt requested and type the
        certified mail number on the letter.

Sample Letter to Delete for Lack of Proof

John Doe
1234 Adam St.
Dallas, TX 75111

January 1, 2004

Manager, Customer Services
Equifax
P.O. Box 740241
Atlanta, GA 30374
Certified Mail #1234 5678 9123 4567 8912
Return Receipt Requested

Dear Manager:

My credit report bearing number 5555444441111 contains an account from XYZ Collection Agency account number 222224444333. Please delete this entry, I was never delinquent or provide copies of signature, agreements, invoices, statements, and notices of delinquencies.

XYZ Collection Agency has failed to verify the account after my formal request of verification of debt as required by law per the enclosed letter.

In accordance with the Fair Credit Reporting Act, a person shall not furnish information relating to a consumer to any consumer reporting agency, if the person has been notified by the consumer that specific information is inaccurate and the information is, in fact, inaccurate. The negative entry is costing me thousands of dollars each year because of adverse reporting.

Your earliest reply is greatly appreciated.

Sincerely,

John Doe

Letter to the Federal Trade Commission for Compliance

You must wait for 45 days before taking the necessary action against the credit bureau. The law allows you to give the credit bureau reasonable time to reply and 30 to 45 days is considered reasonable enough.

You will write to the government and the purpose is to force the credit bureaus to obey the law by deleting the account or proving that the account is yours.

The credit bureau cannot say the account was investigated if it could not provide copies of documentary evidence of obligor's indebtedness, as required by law. Also, report to the authorities that the collection agency does not have proof of documented evidence. You letter to the FTC, the state Attorney General, and the BBB does not need a follow-up letter. Normally, the authorities will begin an investigation immediately and inform you of their actions.

You are now calling on the government to force the credit bureau to delete the entry from your credit report or comply with the law by proof of signature, agreements, invoices, statements, notices of delinquency.

Sample Letter to the FTC for Compliance

John Doe
1234 Adam St.
Dallas, TX 75111

January 1, 2004

Federal Trade Commission
600 Pennsylvania Ave., N.W.
Washington, DC 20580
Certified Mail #1234 5678 9123 4567 8912
Return Receipt Requested

Dear Commissioner:

Credit Report Lack of Proof of Account

I am filing a formal complaint against (XYZ Credit Bureau). I have requested that the credit bureau delete a negative entry on my credit report for the following reasons:

1. The collection agency failed to verify the account
2. The collection agency failed to obtain verification of the debt and send a copy of such verification to the consumer.
3. No one should report inaccurate information to the credit bureau.

It has been more than 45 days since the credit bureau refused to delete the entry or provide evidence that the account is mine from the merchant in the form of copies of signature, agreements, invoices, statements, and notices of delinquency. I am enclosing the letters to the collection agency and the credit bureau for your review. My Social Security number is 123-45-6789 and my telephone number is (123) 456-7890. Please open an investigation into this matter.

Your earliest reply is greatly appreciated.

Sincerely,
John Doe

Letter to the Attorney General and Better Business Bureau for Compliance

After you send your letter to the FTC, write a similar letter to the Attorney General of your state and the BBB of your city. Send your letter by certified mail only and print details of delivery from the Internet.

Negotiating a One-Time Payment

The most important part of this section, negotiating for a one-time, full payment is to agree on the amount you will pay and the collector's agreement to delete the negative entry on your credit report. Nothing less than deleting the negative entry is acceptable. Whatever agreement you make, you do not want a collection agency's name on your credit report.

If the account is yours and the agency replies with an offer, check to see if the cut-off date is close, because the collection agent will reply almost the same day he or she receives your letter. When an agent replies with an offer in the letter, he or she wants you to make the first move. In negotiation, whomever makes the first move loses. The offer might be 70% of the total $500, and with the first move, you're going to use the delayed carrot strategy. Wait 30 days and then reply with an offer. Tell the agent the account is not yours, and that you are still investigating, but in the interim, you are offering $159 (that is about 30% of the amount under investigation).

The offer may be printed at the bottom of the letter with instructions to tear and return the bottom part. If you want to pay the entire amount, do not tear and return the bottom part to the collector, rather send a letter and include the following: today's date, account number, and the certified mail number. Your letter should say, "Dear Manager, I'm sending the enclosed check as agreed for a full and complete payment of the obligation." Also, "By cashing the enclosed check, you agree to delete entries with credit bureaus." Write a check for the amount as you agreed and on the memo line on the check, write, "full payment" and below the line write the certified mail slip number as in the letter. On the back of the check, below the signature line, write, "full payment." Make copies of the check, front and back, and a copy of your letter for your file.

Send your letter by certified mail, return receipt requested and confirm that the number of the certified mail matches with the number on the receipt itself, and the one you wrote on the check.

After you offer $159, which is about 30%, their counter offer might be around 60%. If the cut-off date is not near and you have to wait around five years for the account to expire and delete itself from your credit report, close the deal at 60%, if you have enough cash.

If you agree on full payment, send a letter to the collection agency for signature. You may use the following instructions and facts in writing your letter:

1. Send your letter to the vice president or representative you made the agreement with over the phone. Refer to the date of your discussion.

2. State the amount to which you agreed for full payment. Enclose a stamped, self-addressed envelope.

3. State the fact that the representative promised to delete the negative entries with the credit bureaus and change the account to paid as agreed.

4. After you receive the signed agreement letter, send a money order only with a copy of the agreement by certified mail, return receipt requested. Never send a check to a collection agency.

5. Write on the back of the money order, "Cashing money order constitutes full and final payment of debt."

6. Make a photocopy of the money order, front and back, for your records.

7. Request a copy of the credit report to make sure the entry is deleted.

8. Send your letter by certified mail, return receipt requested and type the certified mail number on the letter.

Sample Letter for a One-Time Payment

John Doe
1234 Adam St.
Dallas, TX 75111

January 1, 2004

Vice President (or representative who you spoke with)
XYZ Collection Agency
4321 Adam Lane
Atlanta, GA 30374
Certified Mail #1234 5678 9123 4567 8912
Return Receipt Requested

Dear Vice President:

I appreciate your time in discussing my account. Per our discussion on January 1, 2004, I agreed to XYZ Collection Agency $75.95 (Seventy-five dollars and ninety-five cents) as a full and final payment on account # 5555554444411112.

In return, within five business days of receiving the payment, you agreed to delete any negative entries associated with this account with the credit bureaus. I will forward a payment of $79.95 as soon as this letter of agreement is signed and returned to me in the enclosed stamped and self-addressed envelope.

Your earliest reply is greatly appreciated.

Sincerely,

John Doe

Agreed and accepted
By_____
Name_____
Date_____

Negotiating Scheduled Payments

Scheduled payments are different from a full payment in that you must agree to a monthly payment for a number of months. The most important advantage of using scheduled payments is cash flow. If you have a tight cash flow, you agree to a monthly payment instead of a one-time payment. Another important point is the collection agency will delete the negative entry when you make your first payment.

There are suitable times when you have to use the scheduled payments. The best time to use scheduled payments is when the collection agency refuses your 30% offer and counter-offers with 70%. You may accept the 70%, but with scheduled payments. The second best time is when the collector flatly refuses your offer without a counter offer. This is the right time to bump up your counter offer with scheduled payments. You don't just start talking about scheduled payments in the early stages of the negotiation. The following are four scenarios that would make you decide between a one-time payment and monthly scheduled payments.

1.   Impending purchase,
        Amount of debt is large

2.   Impending purchase,
        Amount of debt is small

3.   No impending purchase,
        Amount of debt is large

4.   No impending purchase,
        Amount of debt is small

First scenario. Negotiating to pay off a collector now or later will depend on how fast you want the correction made on your credit report. In the first scenario, if you are planning on buying a house within the next six months and the amount of debt is large, it is better to agree to scheduled payments. Maybe pay half of the debt now and schedule the other half for 12 months, if your cash flow allows it. Don't forget that it will take 30 days for the credit bureau to delete the negative information.

Second scenario. In this scenario, you have an impending purchase such as buying a car, you want to clean up your credit report as soon as possible, and the amount of purchase is small. The best thing to do is pay the debt off right away with a discount and not to use scheduled payments.

Write a letter to the collection agency and agree to pay off the debt with the understanding that by cashing your check, they agree to delete the negative entry from your credit report.

Third scenario. It might come to a point when you owe a large amount of debt, but don't have a pressing need to clean up your credit report right away. There is no house to buy or new car to finance; therefore, you have a lot of time from now to the time you need to apply for credit. This is the best time to use scheduled payments with a discount, if possible.

Write to the collector and get him or her to agree to scheduled payments. You will write something such as, "I agree to pay $1,500 as indicated in your letter. I will make payments of $100 for 15 months as full and complete payment of the debt. Upon receipt of the first payment, you agree to delete the entries from my credit report." Write the first check for $100 and on the memo line, write "$100 for 15 months as full payment." On the back of the check, below the signature line, write "$100 for 15 months as full payment." Make copies of the check, front and back, and the letter for your file.

Fourth scenario. This is the best position to be in when you have no impending purchases that would force you to clean up your credit report immediately, and the amount of your debt is small. The choice is yours whether to pay it off right away with a discount, which is the best route if you have enough cash flow, or agree to scheduled payments. If you have a lot of time to wait, spread $500 into 10 months by paying $50 a month.

Money orders and cashier's checks are the best methods of payment to the collection agency. From time to time, you will come across a collection agent who doesn't want to deal with you, especially if your debt is less than $100.

The agent will not reply to your letter or return your call. This is the best agent to deal with. Proceed with the following steps:

1. If the collection agency writes to you as required by law, reply and request the name, address, and phone number of the creditor. Send your letter by certified mail, return receipt requested.

2. If there is no reply, write a follow-up letter and repeat your request, using the same name and address of the creditor. This time, add the fact that the account is not yours. And you want the agent to delete the negative entry, or send you proof of signature, agreements, invoices, statements, and notices of delinquency. Again, send your letter certified mail, return receipt requested. Be sure the number on the returned receipt card matches with the number in your letter.

3. If there is no reply, write letters to the three credit bureaus requesting that the negative entry be deleted because the collection agent did not verify the debt, as required by law.

4. Wait 45 days, if you do get a satisfactory answer from the credit bureaus. Write a simple, formal letter to the FTC, Attorney General of your state, and the BBB for compliance.

5. After compliance, request an updated copy of your credit report to verify the negative entry has been deleted.

Sample Letter for Scheduled Payments

John Doe
1234 Adam St.
Dallas, TX 75111

January 1, 2004

Vice President (or representative who you spoke with)
ABC Corporation
4321 Adam Lane
Atlanta, GA 30374
Certified Mail #1234 5678 9123 4567 8912
Return Receipt Requested

Dear Vice President:

I appreciate your time in discussing my account. This is a summary of our January 1, 2004 discussion. I agree to pay ABC Corporation $160 (one hundred and sixty dollars) every month for 12 months starting January 2004 and ending December 2004 as full and final payment on account number 555544444443333111.

My payment will be mailed to 4321 Adam Lane, Atlanta, GA 30374. If for any reason my payment does not reach your office in any month, the past due amount will be cured in the following months as long as the entire amount is paid in full before December 31, 2004.

In return, within five business days of receiving my first payment, you agree to delete any negative entries associated with this account on my credit report. I will send my first payment of $150 as soon as this letter of agreement is signed and returned to me in the enclosed stamped and self-addressed envelope.

Your earliest reply is greatly appreciated.

Sincerely,

John Doe

Agreed and accepted
By_____
Name_____
Date_____

Chapter 10

Working with Government Agencies

The Federal Trade Commission

Federal and state laws govern consumer credit reporting. The FTC is responsible for enforcement of the federal laws. The commission regulates the actions of the merchants, the collection agencies, and the credit bureaus. You will not have to deal with government agencies after following most of the steps to increasing your credit score outlined in this book, because now you are armed with strategies on working with merchants, collection agencies, and the credit bureaus. I'm including this section for your information. You have this tool at your disposal should you ever need it. I have taken nothing for granted when it comes to your credit rights. When you request a copy of your credit report, the credit bureaus will include a summary of your federal rights under the following headings:

1.   You must be told if information in your file has been used against you.
2.   You can find out what is in your file.
3.   You can dispute inaccurate information with the credit bureaus.
4.   Inaccurate information must be corrected or deleted.
5.   You can dispute inaccurate items with the source of the information.
6.   Outdated information may not be reported.
7.   Access to your file is limited to the general public.
8.   Your consent is required for reports that are provided to employers, or reports that contain medical information.
9.   You may choose to exclude your name from the credit bureaus lists for unsolicited credit and insurance offers.
10.   You may seek damages from violators (to your rights).

All three credit bureaus must list these items as your rights; however, each credit bureau may outline them differently. They will send this information to you with your first credit report package, especially if you request for them to do so. In addition to the federal laws, the bureaus will provide you with a summary of the state laws, as required by your state.

Contacting the Federal Trade Commission

The best and easiest way to contact the FTC is through their Web site. Remember that Web site information is evolutionary. The FTC Web site content may change from time to time, but the basic information is the same. If you don't see any information right away as described below, you may have to click other topics to find what you're looking for. To access the FTC Web site and the related credit laws, use the following steps:

1.   Visit www.ftc.gov.
2.   Click For Consumer on the left-hand side
3.   Click Credit at the left of the table

The Fair Credit Reporting Act (FCRA) authorizes and empowers different federal agencies to enforce consumer laws. Use the following addresses and phone numbers to reach the agencies assigned to answer your questions:

1.   For problems or questions with credit bureaus, merchants, and collection agencies, relating to your credit report, your federal agency contact is as follows:

        Federal Trade Commission – CRC
        600 Pennsylvania Ave., NW
        Washington, DC 20580

        The phone number is 1-877-FTC HELP (1-877-382-4357).

2.   For problems or questions with national banks, federal branches/agencies of foreign banks (with word "National" or initials "N.A." after the bank's name), your federal agency contact is as follows:

        Office of the Comptroller of the Currency
        Customer Assistance Group
        1301 McKinney St., Suite 3450
        Houston, TX 77010

        The phone number is 1-800-613-6743.

3.   For problems or questions with Federal Reserve System member banks (except national banks and federal branches/agencies of foreign banks), your federal agency contact is as follows:
Federal Reserve Board
Division of Consumer & Community Affairs
Washington, DC 20551

The phone number is 1-202-452-3693.

4.   For problems or questions with savings associations and federally chartered savings banks (with word "federal or initials "F.S.B." in the federal institution's name), your federal agency contact is as follows:

Office of Thrift Supervision
Consumer Programs
Washington, DC 20552

The phone number is 1-800-842-6929.

5.   For problems or questions with federal credit unions (with words "federal credit union" in institution's name), your federal agency contact is as follows:

National Credit Union Administration
1775 Duke St.
Alexandria, VA 22314

The phone number is 1-703-518-6360.

6.   For problems or questions with state-chartered banks that are not members of the Federal Reserve System, your federal agency contact is as follows:

Federal Deposit Insurance Corporation
Division of Compliance and Consumer Affairs
Washington, DC 20429

The phone number is 1-877-275-3342 or 1-800-ASK FDIC (1-800-275-3342)

7.   For problems or questions with air, surface, or rail common carriers regulated by former the Civil Aeronautics Board or Interstate Commerce Commission, your federal agency contact is as follows:

Department of Transportation
Office of Financial Management
Washington, DC 20590

The phone number is 1-202-366-1306.

8.   For problems or questions with activities subject to the Packers and Stockyards Act, 1921, your federal agency contact is as follows:

Department of Agriculture
Office of Deputy Administration – GIPSA
Washington, DC 20050

The phone number is 1-202-720-7051.

9.   For problems with or questions about identity theft, your federal agency contact is as follows:

Identity Theft Data Clearinghouse
600 Pennsylvania Ave., NW
Washington, DC 20580

The phone number is 1-877-ID THEFT (1-877-438-4338).

These addresses and phone numbers are subject to change. You may have to call 1-800-555-1212, the 1-800 information line to get the current information. The Washington, D.C., FTC line should be able to give you the regional FTC office.

The FTC is an enforcement agency and should be contacted immediately, in writing, whenever you run into the following problems:

1.   A merchant refuses to send you proof of information.
2.   A collection agency refuses to send you proof of information.
3.   A credit bureau refuses to send you proof of information on public information.
4.   A credit bureau refuses to delete an entry from your credit report because a merchant refuses to send you proof of information.
5.   A credit bureau refuses to delete an entry from your credit report because a collection agency refuses to send you proof of information.
6.   A credit bureau refuses to delete an entry from your credit report because you cannot locate a merchant with an address from the credit bureau.
7.   A credit bureau refuses to delete an entry from your credit report because you cannot locate a collection agency with an address from the credit bureau.
8.   A credit bureau refuses to send you a copy of your credit report after you have paid the applicable fees.
9.   A credit bureau refuses to delete an entry from your credit report because it is outdated.
10.   A credit bureau refuses to delete or correct an entry because it is false or incorrect (i.e., personal information or public information entries).

There are numerous reasons to write the FTC, especially when you know that your rights as a consumer have been violated. As always, when you write the FTC, keep a copy of your certified letter. Your letter should include the following information:

- You name, address, and date indented to the left. You should always staple the certified slip from the post office to the top right of the letter.
- The federal agency's address indented to the left
- The title of your letter (e.g., Compliance Enforcement)
- The reason for your letter (e.g., you want an entry to be deleted because you cannot locate a merchant or a collection agency with an address from the credit bureau).

- Enclose a copy of the letter from the merchant, collection agency, or the credit bureau or in the case of not locating a merchant or a collection agency, a copy of the return-to-sender envelope.

The FTC uses five key Fair Credit Acts to regulate, supervise, and enforce the laws to make sure your rights are not violated. The credit laws are revised from time to time; however, the basic principles are to be preserved. Constituents would like to chip away those areas of the law that make them vulnerable to a lawsuit. But don't worry—all eyes are watching this area of the law. After reading this section, communicating with merchants, collection agencies, and credit bureaus will be so easy. Now you know what to do, when to do it, and how to do it. You should continue to refer back to this section for your rights and how to use them. Steps for accessing the five areas of the Consumer Credit Protection Act are as follows:

1.   Visit www.ftc.gov.
2.   Click For Consumers on the left-hand side.
3.   Click Credit on the left-hand side.
4.   Click Rules & Acts at the top. Among other Acts, you'll see the following:

   a. Credit Repair Organization Act
   b. Equal Credit Opportunity Act
   c. Fair Credit Billing Act
   d. Fair Credit Reporting Act—Home Page
   e. Fair Debt Collection Practices Act—Home Page

5.   Click Credit Repair Organization Act.
      Browse through the Act.

6.   Click Equal Credit Opportunity Act.
      Browse through the Act.

7.   Click Fair Credit Billing Act.
      Browse through the Act.

8.   Click Fair Credit Reporting Act—Home Page.

Click Fair Credit Reporting Act on the left-hand side.
Browse through the Act.
Click the Back arrow button at the top left of the monitor.
Click the Fair and Accurate Credit Transaction Act on the right-hand side.
Browse through the Act.
Click the Back arrow button at the top left of the monitor.

9.   Click Fair Debt Collection Practices Act—Home Page.
Click Fair Debt Collection Practices Act on the left-hand side.
Browse through the Act.
Click the Back arrow button at the top left of the monitor.

The Credit Repair Organizations Act

1.   You have the right not to receive any counsel or advice that is untrue or misleading.

2.   You have the right not to receive any counsel or advice about altering consumer's identification to prevent display of a consumer's credit record.

3.   You have the right not to be defrauded or deceived for offer or sale of services by a credit repair organization.

4.   You have the right not to be charged or made to give money or other valuable consideration before services are fully performed.

5.   You have the right to receive a written statement to dispute inaccuracies on your credit report by contacting the credit bureau directly.

6.   You have the right to receive a written statement that neither you nor any credit repair company has the right to have accurate, current, and verifiable information removed from your credit report.

7.   You have the right to receive a written statement that you can obtain a copy of your credit report from a credit bureau and that you may be charged a fee.

8.   You have the right to sign that you have received these statements from the credit repair organization.

9.   You have the right to sue a credit repair organization that violates the Credit Repair Organization Act.

10.   You have the right to cancel your contract with any credit repair organization for any reason within three business days from the date you sign it.

11.   You have the right to cancel your contract without penalty or obligation before midnight of the third day.

12.   You have the right not to receive any services unless you sign a contract.

13.   You have the right not to receive any services before the end of the third business day from the day you sign the contract.

14.   You have the right to receive written contract that sets out the terms and conditions of payment, including total amount of payment.

15.   You have the right to receive a full and detailed description of the services to be performed by the credit repair organization, including guarantees, estimates, and date of completion of services.

16.   You have the right to cancel by writing, "I, hereby, cancel this transaction, (date) (purchaser's signature).

17.   You have the right not to waive your right and any waiver is considered null and void and you have the right not to be asked to sign a waiver.

18.   You have the right to sue and collect actual damages, the greater of actual damages or any amount paid by you to the credit repair organization.

19.   You have the right to sue and collect punitive damages.

20.   You have the right to sue and collect attorney's fees.

The Equal Credit Opportunity Act

1.   You have the right not to be considered for credit based on your sex, race, national origin, or religion.

2.   You have the right not to be coerced into supplying information on your sex, race, national origin, or religion for the purposes of granting you credit.

3.   You have the right not to be asked if you are divorced or widowed if you are applying as a single for the purposes of granting you credit.

4.   You have the right not be asked of your past marital status if you are applying as single for the purposes of granting you credit.

5.   You have the right not to be asked of your sexual orientation for the purposes of granting you credit.

6.   You have the right not to reveal your medical condition or medical history for the purposes of granting you credit.

7.   You have the right not to be considered for credit based on your age, except in the case of a minor.

8.   You have the right to be told with specificity why you were denied credit or why your credit was canceled.

9.   You have the right to receive this information within a reasonable time period not exceeding 90 days or thereabout.

10.   You have the right to be informed of any credit reporting agency that supplied information that forms the basis for denying you credit.

11.   You have the right to bring legal action against the merchant for infringing on your right.

12.   You the have right to be a part of a class action lawsuit against a merchant you who infringes on your right.

13.   You have the right to sue for actual and punitive damages against any merchant who infringes on your right.

14.   You have the right to report any violations to the Attorney General of your state of residency.

15.   You have the right to allow a mediator to resolve the case and that should not deter you in seeking full legal action.

The Fair Credit Billing Act

1.   You have the right to dispute any false transaction on your billing statement and have the amount be deleted from your statement.

2.   You the have right to dispute any incorrect transaction on your billing statement and have the amount deleted from your statement.

3.   You have the right to receive the corrected copy or copies of your statement from the merchant.

4.   You have the right to receive the reply to your inquiries within a reasonable time period not exceeding 30 days or thereabout.

5. You have the right to receive all supporting documents, as proof if the merchant insists the transaction on the account is yours.

6. You have the right to receive the reply to the proof of transaction within a reasonable time period not exceeding 30 days or thereabout.

7. You have the right to have your bill sent to you within a reasonable time period not exceeding 14 days before the due date.

8. You have the right to change your address at any time and have your bill forwarded to your new address within a reasonable time not exceeding 14 days before the due date.

9. You have the right to not have your account be reported as delinquent for 100 days after you reported false or incorrect transaction on your account.

10. You have the right to have any reported delinquency be deleted from your credit report if you have already reported to the merchant of the false or incorrect transaction.

11. You have the right to have corrected copies of your report be resent to all parties who received the previous copies.

12. You have the right to receive notices of any changes in interest, fees, penalties, and other miscellaneous charges before billing.

13. You have the right to receive any refunds on any duplicate payments and overcharges.

14. You have the right to hold the merchant to any debt settlement he reported on your credit report as agreed.

15. You have the right to sue any merchant for violating your right and participate in a class action lawsuit against any merchant.

16.   You have the right to report to the Attorney General of your state of residency.

17.   You have the right to report to other government entities, including the FTC and your local BBB immediately.

The Fair Credit Reporting Act

1.   You have the right to be informed of your rights at the federal level by the credit reporting agencies.

2.   You have the right to be informed of your rights at the state level by the credit reporting agencies, if mandated to do so.

3.   You have the right to find out what is in your credit file and to appear in person to review the content of your credit report.

4.   You have the right to receive a listing of everyone who has requested your credit report within the last two years, including his or her addresses and phone numbers.

5.   You have the right to receive a copy of your credit report for free if you have been denied credit in the last 60 days.

6.   You have the right to receive a copy of your credit report for free if you are unemployed or on welfare.

7.   You have the right to receive a copy of your credit report for free if your report is inaccurate due to fraud.

8.   You have the right to receive your credit report for a reasonable fee in compliance with prevailing federal and state laws.

9.   You have the right to be told if information on your credit report has been used against you to deny your application for credit, insurance, or employment.

10.   You have the right to be informed of the credit reporting agency whose report was used to deny you credit, including their name, address, and phone number.

11.   You have the right to dispute any inaccurate or negative information in your credit report with the credit reporting agencies.

12.   You have the right to have all sources investigate your dispute and report back to the credit reporting agency or you within a reasonable period of time not exceeding 30 days or thereabout.

13.   You have the right to have your dispute be reinvestigated by the credit reporting agencies with all sources within a reasonable period of time not exceeding 30 days or thereabout.

14.   You have the right to add a brief statement to your credit report if the investigation did not result in any corrections.

15.   You have the right to have the new credit report with brief statement be sent to all parties who received your previous reports.

16.   You have the right to have inaccurate or negative information corrected or deleted from your credit report within a reasonable period of time not exceeding 30 days or thereabout.

17.   You have the right not to have corrected or deleted items be reinserted into your credit report unless the source verifies its accuracy or completeness.

18.   You have the right to be told if an item has been reinserted into your credit report no later than five business days, because the source verifies its accuracy or completeness, and be provided with the name, address, and phone number of the source.

19.   You have the right to dispute any false, inaccurate, incomplete, or outdated items and if it cannot be verified, be deleted from your credit report.

20.   You have the right not to have the inaccuracies still be reported to the credit reporting agencies by the source of information after its investigation.

21.   You have the right to have all outdated information be deleted from your credit report (i.e., any negative or derogatory information that is seven to 10 years old).

22.   You have the right to exclude your name from a credit reporting agency's list for unsolicited credit and insurance offers.

23.   You have the right to receive a toll-free number to opt out indefinitely using your file information for unsolicited offers. Currently, the number is 1-888-5OPTOUT (1-888-567-8688).

24.   You have the right not to have anyone access your credit report, except those that are considering your application like creditors, insurers, employers, landlords, or other businesses.

25.   You have the right not to have your credit report released to your current or prospective employer without your written consent.

26.   You have the right not to have your credit report released to creditors, insurers, or employers without your written consent.

27.   You have the right to be informed of anyone who is ordering your credit report for investigative purposes and to have the nature and substance of the information in the investigative consumer report.

28.   You have the right to bring a suit against a violator of your right and seek both actual and punitive damages.

29.   You have the right to be part of a class action lawsuit against any credit reporting agency that violates or infringes on your rights.

The Fair Debt Collection Practices Act

1.   You have the right not to have a collection agency state to any other person that you owe any debt.

2.   You have the right not to have a collection agency communicate to you by postcard or flyer or any other open communication.

3.   You have the right not to have a collection agency communicate to you in any way on an envelope or telegraph that it is a collector of debt.

4.   You have the right not be contacted by a collection agency after you obtain an attorney.

5.   You have the right not to be contacted at an unusual or inconvenient time or place and can be contacted at a convenient place between the hours of eight o'clock in the morning and nine o'clock at night.

6.   You have the right not to be contacted at your place of employment after you have told a collection agency your employer prohibits all debt collection communication.

7.   You have the right not to be contacted by a collection agency after you notify the agency, in writing, that you refuse to pay the debt or that you wish the collection agency to cease further communication with you.

8.   You have the right not to allow a collection agency to use threats or violence or other criminal means to harm you, your reputation, or your property.

9.   You have the right not to allow a collection agency to use obscene or profane language to abuse or harass you.

10.   You have the right not to allow a collection agency to publish a listing with your name among consumers who refuse to pay debts, except to credit reporting agencies.

11.   You have the right not to allow a collection agency to repeatedly and continuously engage you in conversion intended to annoy, abuse, or harass you.

12.   You have the right not to allow a collection agency to call you without identifying themselves on your caller id.

13.   You have the right not to allow a collection agency to use any false, deceptive, or misleading representation of you.

14.   You have the right not to allow a collection agency to tell you or imply that nonpayment of any debt will result in your arrest, imprisonment, seizure, garnishment, attachment, or sale of your property, except through the normal legal process.

15.   You have the right not to allow a collection agency to use unfair or unconscionable means to collect or attempt to collect any debt from you.

16.   You have the right not to allow a collection agency to collect any amount, including interest, fees, charges, or expenses that is not part of the original debt or expressly authorized in the credit agreement you signed or permitted by law.

17.   You have the right not to give a post-dated check for at least five business days to a collection agency, and when you do, to be informed by the agency from three to 10 days that it intends to deposit such post-dated check.

18.   You have the right not to allow a collection agency to ask you for a post-dated check and threaten you with criminal prosecution.

19.   You have the right not to allow a collection agency to deposit or threaten to deposit a post-dated check before the date on the check.

20.   You have the right to receive, from the collection agency, five days after the initial contact, a notice containing the amount of debt, the name of the creditor, and a statement that you have 30 days to dispute all or part of the debt.

21.   You have the right not to be contacted by a collection agency 30 days after you have informed an agency that you are disputing part or all of the debt until the agency can furnish you with the original copies of transaction or debt.

22.   You have right to have any payment you made be applied to any specific debt you authorizes in cases where there are multiple debts.

23.   You have the right to bring legal action against a collection agency that violates the above rights and seek actual and punitive damages.

24.   You have the right to be a part of a class action lawsuit against a collection agency.

25.   You have the right not to allow a collection agency to falsely misrepresent itself from a branch of the federal or state government.

The Attorney General of Your State

Every time you send a letter to the FTC, send the same letter to the Attorney General of your state. Your letter should be sent by certified mail without return receipt requested. State regulators are sometimes very aggressive in protecting consumers' rights.

Investigation into your complaints could start immediately and you would be assigned to a government representative. Your name would be first on the list to be contacted should there be compensation on a future class action lawsuit. Keep copies of your correspondence to the state regulators in your credit file.

When you request your paid credit report, also request a summary of your state rights. The credit bureaus will include it in your package if state law requires it, but it is important to ask for it anyway.

For example, the credit bureaus are adding the following summaries to the credit report letters sent to Texas residents:

1.   You have the right to obtain a copy of your credit file from a consumer credit reporting agency.

2.   You may be charged a reasonable fee not exceeding nine dollars ($9). (This amount changes from time to time.)

3.   There is no fee, however, if your request for a copy of your credit file is made no later than 60 days after the date on which adverse action is taken against you (date of denied letter).

4.   You have the right to place a "security alert" in your credit file.

5.   You have the right to place a "security freeze" on your credit file.

6.   You have the right to file an action to enforce an obligation of a consumer-reporting agency.

If you don't already have the address and phone number of your state Attorney General's office, you may use the following steps:

- Look in the white pages of your phone book under "Government – State" for the phone number.

- Call the number and get the address and phone number of the department in charge of credit bureau and credit reporting complaints.

- Call the complaint department and find the contact person to whom you will be sending your complaints.

Contacting the Attorney General's office is a serious matter, and your complaint will be treated as a matter of urgency if you can prove that your rights have been violated. The following are samples of the problems that may cause you to seek the Attorney General's help:

1.   A credit bureau refuses to delete an entry from your credit report because a merchant refuses to send you proof of information.

2.   A credit bureau refuses to delete an entry from your credit report because a collection agency refuses to send you proof of information.

3.   A credit bureau refuses to delete an entry from your credit report because you cannot locate a merchant with an address from the credit bureau.

4.   A credit bureau refuses to delete an entry from your credit report because you cannot locate a collection agency with an address from the credit bureau.

5.   A credit bureau refuses to send you a copy of your credit report after you have paid the applicable fees.

6.   A credit bureau refuses to delete an entry from your credit report because it is outdated.

7.   A credit bureau refuses to delete or correct an entry because it is false or incorrect.

Your letter to the Attorney General's office should be brief and precise. You may use the following guidelines:

- Include your name, address, and date, indented to the left

- Include the Attorney General's office address, indented to the left

- Title your letter (e.g., Compliance Enforcement).

- State the reason for your letter (e.g., you want an entry deleted because a credit bureau cannot locate a merchant or a collection agency with an address from the credit bureau).

- Enclose a copy of the letter from the merchant, collection agency, or the credit bureau or, in the case of not locating a merchant or a collection agency, a copy of the return-to-sender envelope.

The Local Better Business Bureau

Becoming a member of a local BBB is a hallmark of a good business relationship with the community. A good name is worth more than a million dollars. Commerce and business transactions in this country depend on trust and one of the first places businesses go to investigate other businesses for that trust is the BBB. When you file a complaint against a merchant or a collection agency with the BBB, you are chipping away at the reputation of that company. The business community avoids dealing with a particular company when it discovers that complaints are filed against that company. It is therefore very important to contact your local BBB anytime a merchant, a collection agency, or a credit bureau is breaking the law.

Anytime you send letters to the FTC and the Attorney General, also send one to the BBB. However, the BBB is not an enforcement or compliance agent as are the FTC and the Attorney General of your state. You should look in the white pages of your phone book to find the phone number to your local BBB office. Call that number and ask for the BBB's address and a contact person. Request that brochures be sent to you. The purpose of brochures is to confirm the address of the BBB. You may use the following format in writing your letter:

1.   Include your name, address, and the date, indented to the left.

2.   Include the BBB's address, indented to the left.

3.   Title your letter (e.g., Consumer Compliant Against [insert the name of the company]).

4.   State the reason for your letter (e.g., the company has sent your name to the credit bureau for a business transaction that the company cannot prove; or a credit bureau refused to delete an entry even though you cannot find the merchant with the address from the credit bureau).

5.   Enclose a copy of the letter from the merchant, collection agency, or credit bureau or, in the case of not locating a merchant or a collection agency, a copy of the return-to-sender envelope.

Consulting with an Attorney

While you are waiting for your reply from the FTC, the Attorney General, and the BBB, you should be talking to an attorney to explore your future options. Most of the time, you will not have to go to court. If you can win by going to small claims court, you can also win before the government agencies reply. The FTC and the Attorney General will make sure the credit bureaus obey the law. The one thing that the credit bureaus respect is the law and they will take appropriate steps to comply with it when confronted with someone who knows his or her rights—this book is designed to give you that knowledge. The first meeting with an attorney can be over the phone to get general information. Most attorneys will give you a free initial consultation.

Look in the phone book for an attorney that specializes in credit and business law. When you call the attorney, find out if you can come in for a free initial consultation. During the meeting, find answers to the following questions:

1.   What is the specialization of the attorney?

2.   How long has the attorney been practicing in the field of specialization?

3.   Has the attorney represented anyone with similar problems?

4.   Was the attorney successful in representing that client?

5.   What options do you have with your case?

6.   How much would it cost to represent you?

7.   What is the attorney's hourly rate?

8.   Would the attorney be working with a senior partner on this case?

9.   What is a senior attorney's hourly rate?

10.   Has the attorney won any cases against a credit bureau?

11.   What is the statute of limitations (the date after which no one can sue you for debt) on promissory notes and revolving and nonrevolving credit?

12.   What is the maximum award on small claim cases you can sue for?

There are numerous other questions you can ask your attorney. Explain your situation. Maybe you have written to a merchant or a collection agency that refuses to reply and you have written to the credit bureau that also refuses to delete the entry on your credit report.

Small Claims Court

Some credit bureau cases are very straightforward. Either the debt is yours or it isn't. All you want is someone to prove to you that the debt is yours. You should go to your local small claims court and file a suit against the merchant, collection agency, or credit bureau, if your right is violated. To go to the small claims court, you must make your case a state issue by using your state rights, which are close to the federal rights. You go to small claims court to talk about state rights and federal court to talk about federal rights.

The key to winning in the small claims court is evidence and overpreparation. Rehearse what to tell the judge. The following may give you a clue on how you would go about collecting your evidence:

- You must have proof that you have written to the merchant or the collection agency, with all your return-to-sender letters.

- You must have proof that the merchant or collection agency refused to send you proof of debt from the letter you received from them.

- You must have proof that the credit bureau refused to delete an entry after you could not find a merchant or collection agency.

Going to court is your last resort. If you follow some simple steps in this book, you will not have to go to court. However, sometimes you can run into a situation where you have to go to court. You must first consult with a competent attorney. Prepare yourself thoroughly if you choose to go to small claims court alone. If you do your homework and review the legal summaries in this section, you will be successful in providing strong evidence and in winning your case.

Every step in this book prepares you for small claims court should you decide to sue a merchant, collection agency, or the credit bureau. Most claims are for $1,000 for the actual damages. When you show up before the judge with letters that the defendant—merchant, collection agency, or credit bureau—ignored your requests for proof of information, you have a good lead in the case.

Chapter 11

Easy Ways to Qualify for Credit

The Personal Data Profile

Increasing your credit score requires the following two simple steps: cleaning your credit report and adding new entries. I'm repeating this statement to make sure you don't forget it by the time you have finished this book. In cleaning your credit report, you are correcting and deleting negative entries; and in adding new entries, you are using specific time-tested strategies to flood your credit report with positive entries. These strategies are your everyday buying habits you never thought about that could radically raise your credit score to the highest score. We have been discussing steps to repair your credit report. Now it's time to talk about ways to enhance or add new entries to your credit report. You can be deleting negative entries and enhancing your credit report at the same time. The information that goes into your credit report comes from the following four sources:

- Your application forms
- Public records
- Merchants
- Collection agencies

In general, most information on your credit report originates from your actions when you apply for credit and make your payments on time, or your inactions when you don't make your payments on time. Therefore, it is possible for you to control the information that goes into your credit report and, as a result, you can control your score. Information you supply to the creditors is very important because it is used for or against you. It is a requirement to provide accurate information about you at all times, but most people fill out applications about themselves from the tops of their heads, thereby supplying conflicting credit information. Creating a personal data profile is important if you plan to present accurate information to all creditors at all times.

You'll need to update and carry your personal date profile with you each time you fill out an application form about yourself. Keep this important profile in a safe and hidden place, because anyone who accesses it can go into your account or steal your identity, if they want to. The profile can come in handy anytime you lose your wallet or purse. All you have to do is pull out your profile and call the merchants to suspend your accounts till you find your wallet or purse.

Following is a sample personal data profile form:

Yourself

Name_____

Social Security number_____

Driver's license_____

Date of birth_____

Phone number_____

Current address_____

Own or rent_____ How long_____

Previous address_____

Own or rent_____ How long_____

Employment

Name of employer_____

Address_____

Date started_____

Work phone number_____

Position_____

Supervisor's name_____

Supervisor's phone number_____

Financial Information

Savings account number_____

Name of bank_____

Address of bank_____

Phone number_____

Checking account number_____

Name of bank_____

Address of bank_____

Phone number_____

First automobile account number_____

Name of lien holder_____

Address of lien holder_____

Phone number_____

Amount financed_____

Monthly payment_____

Current balance_____

Second automobile account number_____
Name of lien holder_____
Address of lien holder_____
Phone number_____
Amount financed_____
Monthly payment_____
Current balance_____

Mortgage account number_____
Name of lien holder_____
Address of lien holder_____
Phone number_____
Amount financed_____
Monthly payment_____
Current balance_____

First credit card name Visa/MC/other_____
Credit card account number_____
Credit card company name_____
Address_____
Phone number_____
Credit limit_____
Monthly payment_____
Current balance_____

Second credit card name Visa/MC/other_____
Credit card account number_____
Credit card company name_____
Address_____
Phone number_____
Credit limit_____
Monthly payment_____
Current balance_____

Other debt_____

Account number_____

Company name_____

Address_____

Phone number_____

Amount financed_____

Monthly payment_____

Current balance_____

Other debt_____

Account number_____

Company name_____

Address_____

Phone number_____

Amount financed_____

Monthly payment_____

Current balance_____

Other debt_____

Account number_____

Company name_____

Address_____

Phone number_____

Amount financed_____

Monthly payment_____

Current balance_____

It is worth repeating that you should complete your personal data profile and keep it hidden in a safe place. You will discover that you are providing similar information to all the merchants when you review your credit report. Most recent applications for credit have been downsized to provide only basic information about you, which is used to pull your credit report for an in-depth analysis of your payment history.

When to Apply for Credit

Having a substantial line of credit is very important, especially if you have a small business or plan to have one in the future. Business debt is considered a good debt and personal debt is considered a bad debt. There are times when it's favorable to apply for credit and they include the following:

1.   When you don't need credit
2.   When the interest rate is low
3.   When you've decreased your debt
4.   When your credit score is high
5.   At the end of the month

When you don't need credit. The best times to apply for credit are when you don't need it. The disadvantage is that you might not be as aggressive as when you have a pressing need and have to have it right away. However, as soon as you have a goal and a purpose for getting a line of credit, the drive and the passion will propel you not to take no for an answer. Additionally, when you don't have a pressing need for credit, you will have enough time to plan ahead and qualify yourself for the loan you want. It is absolutely necessary to decide how much credit you want and the time you want it. Your credit score will go through the roof when you have credit card lines of credit you don't use. Because you don't need credit at this time, you must agree to cut up these credit cards or hide them somewhere after you have charged a transaction of $10 or less. Since you are using these credit lines to increase your credit score, the only time you would call for another card is when you want to start your home business.

When the interest rate is very low. Like everything else, interest rates go through cycles. When the interest rate is at its lowest in a decade—an all time low—this is the time to apply for lines of credit. And because you don't need the credit right away, you must apply for a fixed rate only. Do not accept variable interest of any kind unless it is for business, and even for business, stay with a fixed rate.

When the interest rate is very low, it becomes a buyers market, and nobody wants credit. I have seen loan brokers on commission get a second job, because of bad business—nobody wants loans anymore. This is the best time to grab lines of credit, again with the intention of cutting up these credit cards after you have made your first transaction.

When you've decreased your credit. After you have seen how much you owe creditors, there's nowhere to hide. As soon as a lender pulls your credit report, the debt is now in the hands of the lender. Therefore, it is imperative to plan ahead and decrease your debt before applying for credit.

In other words, you are qualifying yourself before you set foot in the lender's office. By qualifying yourself, your prospect of getting a yes is very high all the time.

When your credit score is high. The government has made it easier for you to receive your credit report once every 12 months. Also, you can request your credit report with score for a small fee from a centralized company, the Vantage Score LLC, created by the three credit bureaus. With the score in hand, you can decide what improvements you need to make before filling out the application for credit. If you see that your credit score is high, apply for credit before any unforeseen circumstances force the score to decrease.

As you can correctly predict, your high credit score means a low or zero percent interest rate on future transactions. Low interest rate means more cash flow to you. As previously mentioned, don't forget to lock in the low or zero percent interest rate on a fixed rate—this cannot be overemphasized.

At the end of the month. As with most transactions that involve commission, the best time to approach the sales person, is at the end of the month. Most commission agents do not meet their quotas toward the end of the month. At the auto dealership, you can tell the sales person you want to meet their monthly quota. That salesperson is allowed to approach more customers first before other sales persons, unless you walk in and specifically ask for a particular person.

This aggressive sales person will have to work with any low offers you present. He or she has to plead on your behalf to the manager to approve the deal. Most of the time, exceptions are made for you to close the sale just because you came at the right time.

How to Qualify for Credit

Generally, there are four reasons any creditor would like to extend to you a line of credit. The following are called the four Cs:

1.   Character
2.   Capacity
3.   Collateral
4.   Capital

Character. Your credit character is one of the most important criteria used by creditors to decide if you would make a good customer. The best place to find out if your credit character is good or bad is your credit report. If you have late payments on all or most of your accounts, few creditors will want to deal with you. You have heard it before "Bad credit is OK, bankruptcy is OK..." as long you are ready to pay through the nose—the highest interest rate. Remember merchants like to extend credit to you if your credit report shows you have had a good payment history—no late payments with a competitor. For example, if you have paid off a furniture store credit, most furniture companies will likely approve your credit.

Capacity. Your current monthly income is a good indicator of your ability to handle additional debt. A creditor will calculate your debt-to-income ratio to see if you will have enough cash flow to deserve more credit. It is very important to calculate this ratio yourself before applying for credit, since you know the creditor is going to do the same. Add your monthly payments and divide the total by your monthly income and multiply by 100. It is good to have between 1% and 20%; this would allow the creditor to find room for an additional 10% of credit.

Collateral. When you borrow money, the creditor wants to make sure you will repay the money by requiring you to pledge some assets. In case of default, the company will be able to sell the assets to recover all or part of the loan. When you buy a house or a car, you are required to pledge the house or the car as collateral.

Capital. Some applications are designed to tell the creditor about other assets you may have, and the amount of net worth you have in those assets. Net worth, sometimes called equity, is the value of an asset minus the amount you owe on it. You can increase your net worth on an asset by increasing the amount of your down payment. Creditors are happy to approve your application if you can put down 20% or more as a down payment.

Any time you are applying for credit, review your four Cs to make sure the creditor will be comfortable with you. If your credit character is not good, increase your capital. Also, if your capacity is not good, increase your collateral.

Some creditors use percentages to determine whether they can extend credit to you or not. The most important task is to use these criteria to judge and qualify yourself first before allowing others to judge or qualify you. Creditors use the following four additional percentage rules to qualify you for credit:

1.   **The 10% rule.** No creditor will want to extend to you a credit line of 10% or more of your monthly income. Let's say your monthly gross income was $1,000, no creditor will want to extend credit to you with a monthly payment of $100 or more. Before you apply for credit, ask yourself, "Am I applying for credit of more than 10% of my monthly income from this one creditor?"

2.   **The 20% rule.** No creditor will want to extend to you additional credit if your monthly payment on debt is already 20% of your monthly gross income, not counting your rent or monthly mortgage payments. Let's say your monthly gross income was $1,000, no creditor will extend to you additional credit if your total monthly payments on other debts are already $200. Do your homework before asking for credit beyond the 20% threshold.

3.   **The 28% rule.** No creditor will extend credit to you for rent or mortgage for more than 28% of your monthly gross income. Again,

let's say your monthly gross income is $1,000, no landlord or mortgage lender will approve your application if the mortgage payment or lease payment are more than $280. By far, this is the most important of the rules. Most people that struggle with money or live from paycheck to paycheck have mortgage payments or rent way beyond 28%.

4.   **The 40% rule.** No creditor will extend credit to you if your total monthly debt, including mortgage or rent is already 40%. This rule assumes that the other 60% will take care of your basic monthly expenses, which sometimes is not even enough. In fact, creditors will say you are fully loaded when they calculate and see you have reached this 40% mark and turn you down automatically. Let's say your monthly gross income is $1,000, no creditor will want to extend credit to you if your total monthly payment on other debts is already $400. Now you know that it's up to you to qualify yourself before lenders disqualify you.

Grouping and Classifying Credit

Generally, there are two types of personal credit, revolving and nonrevolving. Revolving accounts are those you use month after month to buy goods and services and make monthly payments. You can choose to make a minimum payment required by the creditor or make a full payment on the total balance. The creditor sets the credit limit; however, on a secured line of credit, you may set the credit limit by the amount you paid up front. The interest on revolving credit is sometimes higher than nonrevolving and the best way to use a revolving account is to pay off the balance each month. The following are examples of revolving accounts:

<u>Revolving accounts</u>

1.   Credit cards
2.   Department stores
3.   Gas cards

Nonrevolving or installment accounts are those with set monthly payments and a set pay-off date. The agreement may call for you to make fixed monthly payments for a number of months or years, and at the end of that date, the account is paid off. The interest rate on nonrevolving accounts is set for the duration of the loan, and may be renegotiated if you choose to refinance the loan. You can decide your monthly payment and pay-off date, as long as the contract does not have a prepayment penalty clause—and you should never sign a contract with a prepayment penalty clause. The following are examples of nonrevolving accounts:

<u>Nonrevolving accounts</u>

1.   Personal loan
2.   Furniture loan
3.   Jewelry loan
4.   Appliance loan
5.   Electronic loan
6.   Computer loan
7.   Car loan
8.   Boat loan
9.   Equity loan
10. Mortgage loan

There is another way of classifying credit for the purpose of accelerating your credit score—the direct secured and the indirect secured. The purpose of this system is to make sure you never default on any payments. Anyone who develops a habit of consistently using this system will not only see their credit score increase, but will see their cash flow double or triple. The system is invaluable to those who are struggling with managing their finances effectively and efficiently. This system is also beneficial to individuals who have gone through bankruptcy and want to start over—with no more mistakes.

In a direct secured, the creditor asks you to deposit a certain amount of money for a particular line of credit. For example, a credit card company will ask you to deposit $500 for a $700 line of credit. In other words, you are partly prepaying to the company before you start charging on your credit card. If you really think about it, there is nothing out of the ordinary about paying cash before receiving goods. This practice is generally called the "pay and charge" rule.

With indirect secured credit, instead of depositing money first with the credit card company, you open a checking account—called "prepaid." This is just an ordinary checking account; prepaid means any money deposited into this account is used to pay off a specific debt. Every month, you make the monthly payment from the "prepaid" checking account. Let's continue with the following example: You first open a separate checking account and deposit $500 or $1,000 in that account. Then, you go and buy furniture on credit. When you receive your bill from the furniture company, you write a check from the checking account. It's as simple as that, and your good credit transactions are reported month after month to the credit bureau.

The same principle can be used in purchasing anything on credit. If you want to avoid paying interest and at the same time boost your credit score, look for companies that sell "same as cash" for a certain period of time. For example, furniture, appliance and computer stores have "same as cash" no interest for two to three years. These companies are betting you will default on your monthly payments or not pay it off within the set period of time, in which case they slap you with a 20% or more interest rate. You will not fall for this trick because you have already saved up the money in your prepaid checking account. Guess what will happen to your credit report after you've used this system over and over? Your credit score will go through the roof because you are building a good payment history. Advantages in using the "pay and charge" rule include the following:

1.   You have saved up the monthly payment on the debt.

2.   You will never pay interest on debts because you are paying them off at the end of the month. For credit cards and installment credit such as furniture credit, you are making your own payments not the minimum payment as suggested by the creditor, thereby paying them off within the free interest rate period.

3.   You have good payment history from different household items you bought.

4. Your good payment history is being recorded by the credit bureaus, which accelerates your credit score to the maximum.

5. You are now a trusted person who can ask and receive higher lines of credit from creditors at any time.

6. Because you have a high score, you pay little or zero percent interest on new cars and prime rate on mortgage, which translates into good cash flow month after month. Many households are using the "pay and charge" rule to buy all items, including cars, trucks, and homes.

Chapter 12

Adding New Entries to Your Credit Report

Adding New Entries to Your Credit Report

The basic principle of adding new entries to your credit report is to make sure you do not pay cash to companies when you can use the same cash and pay for credit purchases so that credit histories are reported to the credit bureaus. We have touched on this principle in the previous section, now we are going into detail about how to make it work for you. One of the problems with credit is sometimes consumers overextend themselves with regard to available cash. To avoid this problem, first deposit the cash in a checking account and then pay the credit or loan company from the cash in the bank.

By Credit Card Account

A credit card is one of the most powerful tools in money management; the problem is that many people think that a credit card is money. When you see a credit card as secured money, you will never have trouble paying it off at the end of the month. In other words, you have the cash already in the bank before you go out and charge on your credit card. This is what we call the "pay and charge" rule—putting money in the bank and then charging your expenses.

If you already have a credit card with one or more late payments, the best action is to repair the late payment entry on your credit report before applying for another credit card. If by any chance you cannot repair the negative entry, immediately open another credit card account with the same credit card company for a minimum line of credit, and then close the old credit card account.

The only time you replace an account with the same account is when you're dealing with the same company. When you are dealing with two different companies, do not replace an account with the same type of account. For example, let say it is impossible for you to delete a negative credit card entry on your credit report, don't approach another credit card company for a credit card because the company will see you've defaulted on a similar account and may deny you. Instead, wait until the account has expired from your credit report before applying for a credit card. You should replace the credit card with jewelry credit or furniture credit. In other words, if you have a negative credit card entry, open a furniture or jewelry account of equal amount to neutralize the effect of the negative entry. This is another way of telling prospective merchants, though you made a mistake in the past, you are beginning a new credit history.

If you do not have a credit card, the first place to go to is your bank. If you've had three or more nonsufficient funds (NSFs) on your checking account in one year, I don't encourage going to your bank but opening another account at a credit union. After a month or two, go back and apply for a credit card. Be sure you don't have any NSF within that period. Apply for the minimum line of credit. Your objective is to start small and gradually increase your available credit. To the credit bureau, a $100 line of credit with no late payments has a higher credit score value than a $1,000 line of credit with one late payment.

If you are denied a credit card by your bank or credit union, go to the loan officer and ask for a secured credit card. You will have to deposit cash for the minimum line of credit in your savings account, and the credit union will freeze the cash for your new credit card.

You may use the following steps to establish your credit card account:

1.   If you have a credit card with late payments, open a new account with the same credit card company and in few months, close the old account with late payments.

2.   If you don't have a credit card, go to your bank or credit union where you currently have an account and apply for one. Make sure the bank or credit union reports to all three major credit bureaus.

3.   If you don't have an account with a bank or credit union, go to a credit union only and open a savings account. Make sure the credit union reports to all three major credit bureaus.

4.   After a month or two, go back to the credit union and ask for the minimum line of credit on a credit card, and apply for a credit card on

that minimum. Credit unions are very friendly in granting credit cards if you have a fair credit history.

5. If you are denied a credit card because of bad or no credit history, ask for a secured credit card, and deposit cash for the minimum credit line in a savings account to be frozen for a credit card.

6. Ask the loan officer, "If I make all your credit card payments on time, how long will it take to apply for an unsecured credit card?" Probably, he or she will tell you six months to one year.

7. You may designate this account to buying food and gas only. You must ask the loan officer to set up the system to decline a transaction anytime you reach your credit limit. Carry other forms of payment with you at all times, because if you are over the credit limit by even one dollar, you will be charged overdraft fees. You must find a company who can honor this request and most companies do.

8. After six months or one year as specified by the loan officer, go back and open an unsecured credit card, thereby freeing up the cash in your savings account.

9. Ask for your cut-off date. Make your high dollar purchases immediately within or after the first five days after the cut-off date, that way you have a longer time to receive the bill and more time to pay it. If you make high dollar purchases right before the cut-off date, you will get the bill on those purchases immediately or be forced to pay accrued interests.

By Jewelry Store Credit Account

What if the Christmas season or other occasions are coming soon and you want to surprise your loved ones? Wait before you hand over the cash or check to the cashier and ask, "Can I finance this purchase?" The sales person would like to make the sale, and therefore will call the head office and tell them a cash customer wants to finance a purchase. Your engagement ring, wedding ring, and anniversary ring—all can be bought on credit, while you deposit the cash in the checking account to be used to pay off the credit. It would be to your advantage to apply for the jewelry store credit in the same month you applied for the department store credit card. You may use the following steps to implement your jewelry store credit account:

1.   Go to a jewelry store three months after you receive your credit card.

2.   Make sure the store does its own financing. Some finance companies are hard to work with and their interest rates are very high.

3.   Make sure the jewelry store reports to the three major credit bureaus.

4.   Select the jewelry you want to pay cash for. Before you give cash or a check to the sales person, ask if you can finance the jewelry.

5.   The purpose is to get credit for something you were going to pay cash for.

6.   Finance the jewelry for one year and make sure there is no prepayment penalty. Deposit the cash you were going to pay into the "prepaid" checking account as soon as possible.

7.   Use your personal data profile to complete the application form to make sure you are using the correct information. Remember you are the one that supplies most of the information on your credit report.

8.   Ask for the maximum number of grace period days allowed after your payment is due, that way the merchant will not report you to the credit bureau for being charged with late fees.

9.   Ask the jewelry store if it can withdraw your monthly payments directly from your checking account.

By Furniture Store Credit Account

You may have to apply for a furniture store credit account in the same month you applied for the jewelry store credit account, so that after two years both inquiries will drop from your credit report. Furniture store credit is one of the easiest accounts to obtain, followed by mattress store credit. I cringe every time I see someone write a $200 or more check to a furniture store. All I'm thinking about is the number of credit score points they are losing. What if every major purchase in your household is an entry on your credit report, how many positive entries could you have? If you are a young family or are starting over after bankruptcy, this is the best way to guarantee that all future entries on your credit report will be positive.

Walk through your house or apartment and count the number of items you paid cash for, or should I say you lost credit score points on. Furniture is one of my favorite items because it is replaced every three to seven years. Don't throw away your good credit score, deposit the cash in your "prepaid" checking account and get one year same as cash, interest-free credit. Furniture companies have the highest interest-free period, take advantage of it and make sure it is paid off before the end of the contract period—with the cash you were going to give to the company. You may use the following steps to implement your furniture store credit account:

1.   Go to a furniture store the same month you apply for the jewelry store account.

2.   Make sure the furniture store does its own financing. Some finance companies are hard to work with and their interest rates are very high.

3.   Make sure the furniture company reports to the three major credit bureaus.

4.   Ask if they will give two years or more free interest "same as cash" financing. Make your payments on time because they are betting you will miss payments and be slapped with a late and higher interest rate.

5.   Ask the sales person for the minimum purchase to open an account. The goal is to buy your household items on credit and make payments that are reflected as good payment history rather than paying cash to the furniture store with no points on your credit report.

6.   Find an item around the minimum purchase price and fill out the application form.

7.   Use your personal date profile to complete the application form to make sure you are using the correct information. Remember you are the one that supplies most of the information on your credit report.

8.   Ask for the number of grace period days after your payment is due and make sure it is written on your contract. Have the sale person underline it on the contract.

9.   If you have cash to buy furniture, stop and deposit that cash in your "prepaid" checking account, and finance the furniture for one year. Make sure there is no prepayment penalty. Have the sales person underline it on the contract.

10. You may make a three-month payment at one time to reduce your balance. Remember to spread the balance, but not below the minimum monthly payment the furniture company requested.

11. Ask the furniture company if it can withdraw your monthly payments directly from your checking account.

By Department Store Credit Account

After you have successfully managed your credit card, jewelry store credit account, and furniture store credit account, you are ready to venture out into the world of department store credit cards. If you already have a department store credit card with late payments, repair it or open another account with the same store and later close the account with the late payments. Most department stores will not require you to deposit funds with the store first before making purchases.

Consumers get into big problems with a department store credit card because they see the store credit card as money instead of credit. The best approach is to first save the money and then charge the item on your credit card. It is important to designate your department store credit card for clothing, shoes, and accessories only, and not pay for these items with your Visa or MasterCard. To stop buying clothes for one year, all you have to do is remove your department store credit card from your purse or wallet. The key to managing your credit card accounts is to have the cash flow to pay for your purchases at the end of the month. Your goal is to have an impeccable credit history that translates into the highest credit score. You may use the following steps:

1.   Go to your favorite department store.

2.   The key is to accelerate your credit score by buying clothes, shoes, and other things you would normally pay for with cash.

3.   Ask the customer service representative if the department store reports to all three major credit bureaus. Get it in writing, if possible.

4.   Ask for the minimum credit limit, if there is one, and apply it.

5.   Ask the representative how long it takes to review your account for a credit increase, and make sure you have the representative write it down for you on the agreement that you will take home with you. Most department stores will make credit enhancements every six months. At this time, you will receive one of the following: a lower interest rate, an increased line of credit, no annual fees, refunds on late payments, or a late payment cancellation with the credit bureau. All credit card companies offer these enhancements—it is a little secret few people know. Therefore, you must ask for credit enhancement on all your credit cards every six months or find out how long it takes to get.

6.   The idea is to continue to get an increased credit limit with each review, when you don't need credit. You should only charge 20% of your credit limit each month. You receive a very high credit score on an account if you have a high credit limit with a small amount owed.

7.   You may designate this account for buying clothes, shoes, and accessories only. It is very important to manage your money efficiently; this is one way of doing that.

8.   If you plan to use your department store credit card, prepay your charges by depositing cash into your "prepaid" checking account.

9.   As you practice the "pay and charge" rule, make sure that when you receive your department store card bill, there is enough money in the bank to pay off the balance.

10.   Use your personal data profile to complete the application form to verify that you are using the correct information.

11.   Ask for the number of grace period days without reporting a late payment to the credit bureau, not without paying a higher interest rate of 21% for the month. Most stores have a five-days grace period after the payment is due. Have the sales person underline or write it on the contract. Mail the payment; don't take it to the store. The day you take your payment is always before your cut-off date. Don't fall for that trick. You may look and browse around the store, just come back after the cut-off date and buy the merchandise. As explained previously, if you're tricked into buying before the cut-off date, you have only a few days to pay, but if you come back and buy the merchandise immediately after the cut-off date, you have almost a month to pay for that merchandise.

12.   If you really have a cash flow problem, write all your checks on the first day of the month and only mail it one week before the due date, that way you don't forget to write checks for any bills.

13.   Ask for your cut-off date. You must make most of your purchases immediately after the cut-off date, not before the cut-off date as explained previously.

By Appliance Store Credit Account

This is one of the easiest ways to add positive entries to your credit report. Most households buy all kinds of appliances almost every year. In those instances, the majority of customers walk into the appliance store and hands over their hard-earned cash to a store clerk without getting any entry on their credit report. All they have to do is deposit that cash into the "prepaid" checking account. I use the words "prepaid" checking because the idea is for you to open a separate checking account just for this purpose; remember your objective is to have the highest credit score. You need a separate bank account, because if you deposit this cash in your regular checking account, there is temptation to dip into the cash. But when you have a "prepaid" checking account, the temptation is minimized.

Can you look around your house and count the number of appliances you paid for with cash? When you open an appliance store credit account from your favorite store, any time you want to buy something for cash, charge it on your account, pay for it and get credit on your credit report. Remember this is not a credit card; you are looking for a store that will give you 90-180 days same as cash with no interest. That way you can make the minimum payment or spread it out from three to six monthly payments without paying interest. The following are the steps you would use to establish and manage your appliance store credit account:

1.   Say you've saved up to $200 to buy an appliance for your household. Go to your neighborhood appliance store and select the appliance you've wanted to buy.

2.   Ask the cashier if you can finance the appliance. If the answer is yes, go tell the sales person that you've decided to open an account with the store so you can always buy on credit.

3.   Before you fill out the application, make sure the store reports to the three major credit bureaus. Ask a manager if the salesperson is not sure.

4.   Ask for the minimum credit limit, if there is one, and apply for it or if there is no minimum, apply for the exact amount of the appliance.

5.   You may designate this account for buying all appliances and related merchandise, so that when you remove the card from your wallet or purse and hide it, you won't have to use it.

6.   If you plan to use your appliance store credit card, prepay your charges by depositing cash into your "prepaid" checking account.

7.   Use your personal date profile to complete the application to make sure you are giving out the same information all the time.

8.   Ask for the number of days grace period, most stores have a five-day grace period after the payment is due. Have the sales person underline or write it on the contract. Mail your payment; don't take it to the store.

9.   You can always go to another appliance store and repeat the same process. In fact, when you've finished paying on the first item, open another account and use the same process. After the second item is paid off, go to another appliance store and repeat the process.

By Electronic Store Credit Account

I'm discussing these accounts separately so that you'll remember to have them on your credit report. Most clients forget they can add these accounts to their credit report. Are you adding new entries with an electronic store credit account? This is one of my favorites. It is different from the appliance store credit account, because only a few items will qualify as home appliances. However, a lot of items will qualify as electronic appliances. If you have kids, the number of new entries you will get on your credit report from an electronics store is unbelievable. Before your children run off to buy that Nintendo, have them give you the cash; then apply for credit for that item and have the cash deposited into the "prepaid" checking account where you will make the monthly payment until it is paid off.

Look at all the electronic items in your household. Every item is almost like a positive entry on your credit report. Now, you know how some consumers have the highest credit score and others have the lowest. You can also teach your kid this system, and once it becomes a part of their psyche—it will stay with them forever. The following steps constitute the process of opening an electronic store credit account:

1.   When you've decided on an electronic item you want to buy and have saved up the cash, go to an electronic store and select the item you want to buy.

2.   Ask the cashier if you can finance the electronic item. Tell the sales person that you've decided to open an account with the store so that you can always buy on credit.

3.   Ask a manager if the store reports to the three major credit bureaus.

4.   Ask for the minimum credit limit, if there is one, and apply for it or if there is no minimum, apply for the exact price of the electronic item.

5.   You may designate this account for buying all electronics and related items, so that when you remove the card from your wallet or purse and hide it, the temptation of using the card diminishes.

6.   If you plan to use your electronics store credit card, prepay your charges by depositing cash into your "prepaid" checking account.

7.   Use your personal data profile to complete the application to make sure you are using the correct information. Remember, you are the one that supplies most of the information on your credit report.

8.   Ask for the number of grace period days. Most stores have a five-day grace period after the payment is due. Have the sales person underline or write it on the contract. Mail your payment; don't take it to the store.

9.   You can always go to another electronics store and use the same
        process.

As an Authorized User

The easiest way to add 5-10 years of good entries to your credit report, thereby
increasing your credit score, is to find a relative or friend who you will add to
your account as an "authorized user." That way the company will report the
good credit activities from one credit card to multiple Social Security numbers
and multiple credit reports. If you allow your friend or relative to take your
cash and put entries on their credit report, they should, in return, allow you to
be named as an "authorized user" on that same credit account. Don't use this
process with someone you don't trust completely or with someone with money
problems. Parents can use this powerful method to create the highest credit
scores for their children or anyone else. The system works as follows:

1.   You see a family member or friend who has credit problems, and you
        are willing to help them by adding new entries to their credit report.

2.   All your family member or friend has to do is save up to $100 and give
        it to you, which you will deposit into a "prepaid" checking account.

3.   You charge the merchandise they wanted on your name and make the
        family member or friend an "authorized user" to the account.

4.   You give them the merchandise and keep the cash in the bank.

5.   You make the payments until you pay off the merchandise with the cash
        in the bank.

6.   If you can repeat this process on five items for $100, you have five new
        positive entries on your account and the family member or friend's
        credit report. That's a lot of points on their credit report.

7.   Greatest of all, if you have an excellent credit score, you can add your children on your accounts and this will give them almost the same score you have.

By Personal Loan

Another way to increase the activities and entries on your credit report is to apply for a personal loan. This is the most important way to add entries to your credit report, according to the credit bureaus, because it will earn you more points than other strategies, except mortgage and auto payments. In fact, if you have 10 negative entries or more, this should be your first step in repairing your credit report. It is advisable to repeat the process with a higher amount with the same credit union or another one every year for three years. You want to show both revolving and nonrevolving entries on your credit report. A personal loan is one of the easiest ways to show a nonrevolving account on your credit report. This is one of the best uses of your tax refund or any lump sum of money you may receive. After the process is completed, you will still have your tax refund minus nine to 12 months interest on the loan. You may use the following steps:

1. Go to your neighborhood credit union or bank.

2. Ask whether the credit union or bank reports to all three major credit bureaus.

3. Open a savings account on the minimum amount the bank or credit union can lend on a personal loan.

4. Apply for a personal loan for the amount in your savings account and ask the loan officer to freeze your savings account and use it as collateral for the personal loan.

5. Deposit your loan check into the savings account. Now you have your original savings and your loan money all in the same account.

6. Do not buy any insurance that may be offered to you on the loan.

7. Borrow the money for a period of one year and pay it off in nine months. You will continue to make your monthly payments and in the ninth month, withdraw cash from your savings account and pay off the loan. Also, if you continue to make your payments while you still have your loan check in the savings account at the end of the loan period, you will have saved all the money in your savings account. This is called forced savings.

8. Ask the loan officer that if you make your payments on time, how long it would take to apply for an unsecured personal loan.

9. Tell the loan officer you want the bank or credit union to withdraw the monthly payment each month directly from the savings account—make sure it is set up as you requested.

10. You don't have to worry about making the payment yourself each month. All you need to do is open your monthly statement and make sure the balance is going down steadily.

11. Make sure there is no prepayment penalty. Ask the loan officer to underline it on the contract.

Chapter 13

The Basics of
the Credit Score

Who Created the Credit Score?

T he credit bureaus want you to believe they are the architects of the credit score, but without your purchases on credit, there is no credit report or credit score. Over the years, a lot has happened to the numbering system. The credit bureaus have different names for the credit score: Equifax calls it Beacon, Experian calls it Experian FICO, and TransUnion calls it Empirica. Recently the three credit bureaus came together and concocted a new name for credit score—VantageScore. Following is what it looks like:

1.   901—990   Perfect
2.   801—900   Excellent
3.   701—800   Good
4.   601—700   Fair
5.   501—600   Poor

The only thing that stays the same in the credit score business is you—the owner of the credit score! Everything changes all the time! Change is the only commodity that keeps the credit bureaus in business. They change their names, addresses, phone numbers, and yes, your credit score in the blink of an eye—if you're not watching them. The only thing that counts as far as the merchants are concerned is money—lots of money! One problem with the credit report is that it does not tell a merchant if your income has increased or not, until you apply for credit and declare your current income. Your income may have changed tremendously and the merchant will have to determine your capability to handle additional debt to be able to extend to you more credit. The credit bureaus do not have this information and cannot stop the merchant from extending to you additional credit if your income has increased. Sometimes, merchants ignore the credit score and say something such as, "We don't serve the credit bureaus; the credit bureaus serve us..."

The credit bureaus want you to think they are the ones calling the shots when, in fact, they are not—not at all—you are! Actually, you are the one creating the credit score and the credit report. The credit bureau industry does not want you to know this; they want you to believe they are the ones creating your score. Remember that without you, there is no credit score. If you decide never to buy anything on credit, there will not be any credit report or score on you. You shouldn't be running scared of the credit bureaus either—rather deal with them—it's your report and your score. When you make good decisions, your score goes up and when you make bad decisions, your score goes down—it's all in your power. What's important to you is not to concentrate on the report, but to make good credit decisions, and watch your report every year to make sure nothing is added or subtracted without consent. Following are the previous addresses of the three major credit reporting agencies. Notice that these are physical addresses and not post office boxes, which are susceptible to change. Guess what? I don't trust these addresses, either, because they may change by the time you finish reading this book:

1.   Equifax CSC
        652 N. Sam Houston Pkwy E, Suite 133
        Houston, TX 77267

        Equifax CSC
        652 North Belt E, Suite 133
        Houston, TX 77267

2.   Experian
        701 Experian Pkwy
        Allen, TX 75013

3.   TransUnion
        1561 E. Orangethorpe Ave.
        Fullerton, CA 92831

        TransUnion
        25249 Country Club Blvd.
        North Olmsted, OH 44070

To contact the credit bureaus, never write to them unless you have their current addresses from a merchant who denied you credit or from the Internet. You must print the credit bureaus' addresses to keep written proof in your file. Also, you must always write, not call, the credit bureaus, because you want to document all contact with the credit bureaus. You would feel awful upon receiving return-to-sender mail from the credit bureaus after you had spent money on registered or certified letters, because you used a wrong address, given to you from a credit bureau.

When you write to the credit bureaus, they will reply to you from one of their local offices near you, and they change these local offices so you won't keep up with their shenanigans. When they have deleted information from one office, they will close that office and open another office in another city just to reinsert all the information they have deleted from the previous office. That is why you must have a binder to keep track of the deleted entries from your credit report.

Who Uses the Credit Score?

If you want to know everything about a consumer, the first and the best place to go is to his or her credit report. Any business can now request a consumer's credit report and get it—with ease. After months of lobbying, Congress has decided to even make it a law, and it says, "anyone who has legitimate business purpose" can request your credit report. If you don't have any business with a consumer, and you want his or credit report, find a way to get the consumer to fill out an application. Now you know why you should never fill out an application that comes to you unsolicited or as junk mail—it's a set up!

The following business categories are currently using the services of the credit bureaus and looking into your credit report even without your knowledge:

1.   Employers
2.   Mortgage lenders
3.   Auto finance companies
4.   Insurance companies
5.   Landlords
6.   Credit card companies
7.   Department stores
8.   Furniture stores
9.   Utility companies

10.   School loan lenders
11.   Collection agencies
12.   Judgment creditors
13.   Government agencies
14.   Businesses
15.   Banks and savings and loan companies

The list is endless. The principle to remember is that whenever you are conducting a business transaction with anyone that involves credit, they have the right to pull your credit report. If you don't want your credit report pulled, do not fill out a credit application.

How Much is a Low Score Costing You?

When you think about credit scores, you think about one word—interest. And when you think about interest, you think about one word—drainage. Yes, thousands of dollars are draining each year from your financial tank. What if you have a big tank of water sitting in your back yard and one day you come home only to see water pouring out of a hole in that tank, and all your belongings floating in the floodwaters? Would you just stand there and do nothing? I don't think so! You would rush to the tank and do everything to plug the drain.

The same thing is happening with your financial tank. Don't just sit there and watch the flood of interest payments pouring out of your cash tank. It is high time you plugged the drain—and the time is now! How long will you sit there and continue to pay 20% in interest, while others are paying 0%? How long will you sit there and watch merchants toasting and splurging over your credit and financial ignorance? There are two ways of destroying this dragon-headed monster called interest. The first one is by paying cash for everything you buy—you don't have to do that, especially now that we are almost becoming a cashless society. The second is by paying zero percent interest on anything you buy on credit. Kings pay zero percent interest, princes and princesses pay prime, and paupers pay the market interest rate, or any rate the merchant decides to gouge from you. If you must pay interest on anything at all, you must think about one word—prime. This is the interest rate banks charge their very best customers—what princes and princesses pay.

Let's look at some numbers. Once a merchant requests and receives your credit report, a certain interest rate is quoted to you based on your credit score. This is where the merchants are getting the interest rate they are quoting to you.

	Your Credit Score	Interest Charged
1.	901—990	2% or less
2.	801—900	4% or less
3.	701—800	6% more or less
4.	601—700	8% more or less
5.	501—600	10% or more

I will not bore you with compound interest calculations. However, you need to know that interest rates are your number one financial enemy. Interest rates can also be your number one financial friend if you are the one collecting the interest payments. The good news is that your enemy is very easy to defeat, if you know how. The book in your hands will give you the know-how on defeating your financial enemy—it's very easy. Let me show you how dangerous interest rates are when buying anything on credit. For example, if you have a credit score of 645, your interest is about 7%. And if, for example, you are going to buy a house that costs $200,000 over 30 years, your monthly payments will be $1,330.60 and your total payments will be $479,016. What if you clean up your credit report and move your score to 785? Now the interest rate the lender will charge you will be about 4%. Your monthly payments will now be $954.83 and your total payments reduced to $343,738.80; that is $135,277.20 in savings. If you add $148.98 to the original monthly payments, you will pay off your house in 15 years instead of 30. The feeling of owning a $200,000 home, free and clear in 15 years is incredible—and that's what smart people are doing right now. I could use up pages telling you how low credit score and high interest rate is picking your pocket year after year—it's time to pull the plug on your number one financial enemy.

What is the moral of this example? You must bargain when it comes to interest rates—and a high credit score will make the negotiation a lot easier than you think. Do not accept the first interest rate that is quoted by a merchant. You should shop around, the merchants expect you to. Before you buy a car or any high value asset, find out your credit score and know the approximate interest rate you are going to pay. Certainly, before you go to buy a house, increase your score by following the steps outlined in this book, it's worth it—a thousand times over!

What Information Affects Your Credit Score?

The information that goes into your credit report comes from three sources, your applications, subscribers, and public records. Subscribers are customers of credit bureaus who are willing to pay the credit bureaus to give and receive credit information about you. They include collection agencies, credit card companies, department stores, banks, savings and loan companies, mortgage lenders, car dealerships, employers, insurance companies, and a host of other businesses.

From time to time, an attorney who has a judgment against you may report it to the credit bureau. At other times, credit bureaus will use their own employees or a third party agent to update their records about public information. Agents will search court records for information on bankruptcy, foreclosures, tax liens, and other judgments on individuals and report back to the credit bureaus. Information that goes into your credit file can affect your score positively or negatively.

It is very important to remember that your credit history is reviewed at two levels, first, at the credit bureau level where a score is assigned to your report and, second, at the merchant level, where the actual credit request is granted. The merchant level is more important than the credit bureau level, because a credit decision is partially, not totally, based on your credit score.

The quality of the businesses on the credit report is very important to the reviewer. A car loan from a Jaguar dealership is more favorable than a car loan from your neighborhood finance company. A $200 furniture loan from Ethan Allen is more favorable than a $1,000 credit from an interest hungry fly-by-night finance company. What would you think about a credit card from Chase

Bank compared to one from a loan shark credit card company from a remote city or town?

Your credit report, reviewed at both credit bureau and merchant levels, would be affected positively by the following information:

1.   Many paid off installment accounts with paid as agreed or paid satisfactorily status comments (e.g., automobile, furniture, jewelry, computer, entertainment, appliances, etc.).

2.   Many zero balance revolving accounts with large credit limits, eg credit cards, department stores, gas cards, etc. You should never charge more than 20% of your credit limit.

3.   Four or fewer low balance, high credit limit installment account entries with paying as agreed comments

4.   Four or fewer low balance, high credit limit revolving account entries with paying as agreed comments

5.   A low debt-to-income ratio—total monthly payments divided by total monthly income

6.   A low debt-to-credit limit ratio—total monthly payments divided by total credit limit

7.   Long history of credit report with no late payments or delinquencies, just paid as agreed or paying satisfactorily.

8.   Absence of negative public records on credit report

9.   Absence of negative collection accounts on credit report

10.   Absence of late payments or delinquent accounts

11.   A few inquires on your credit report, not more than four inquiries in one year

12.   Account closed by customer's request and not by merchant

13.   The quality of companies and businesses on your report

14.   How you paid on a similar business being reviewed by a merchant (e.g., how you paid on your last furniture credit).

15.   Long years of being a customer to a competitor, especially if the account was just closed by the customer. The longer you are with a certain credit card company, the more favorable.

16.   Number of years on your current job or years in business by yourself

The opposite of most information outlined above would cause your credit score to be lower. However, reviewing your credit report at both the credit bureau and merchant levels would be affected by the following negative entries:

1.   Bankruptcy
2.   Tax liens
3.   Judgments
4.   Repossession
5.   Voluntary surrender
6.   Charge-off
7.   Paid Charge-off
8.   Collection
9.   Paid collection
10.   Delinquent
11.   Number of account past due
12.   Accounts closed by creditor's request
13.   Credit counseling companies
14.   Too many new accounts
15.   Excessive number of inquiries
16.   The quality of companies and businesses on your report
17.   How you paid on a similar business being reviewed by a merchant
18.   Few months of being a customer to a competitor and the account is still open

19.   Few months on current job or a new business owner
20.   Quality of current job and quality of your employer

The following business activities are not listed on your credit report. However, the collection policies of these merchants are more aggressive than other businesses. If you owe them for a number of months more than they can handle, they will first cut off your services, and then send you a final bill. If you do not pay the final bill within 30 days, they will report your account to the credit bureaus. Whatever you do, keep the final bill in a safe place until you pay the final bill or have the entry deleted from your credit report—seven years from the date of delinquency—which is the date on your final bill.

The following activities are nonreportable to the credit bureaus:

1.   Bad checks (which are reported to Chex System)
2.   Apartment rent payments
3.   Telephone bills
4.   Cable bills
5.   Gas and electric bills
6.   Employment dismissal
7.   Magazine subscription payments
8.   TV commercial payments without credit check
9.   Internet monthly fees
10.   Storage fees

Do You Want to Design Your Credit Report?

Designing your own credit report does not mean creating a new identity or doing anything illegal or unethical with your credit report. It is about being in control and making sure all credit activities are reported completely and accurately on your credit report. It means you creatively select the best businesses you want to show on your credit report.

You are going to create a million-dollar credit report since the whole world is looking at it anyway. It involves being in control of whom you do business with and carefully selecting those business names that would tell the whole world you are in a "class by yourself." Right now, you are just spending your money with anybody and everybody, instead of concentrating your spending power on a few quality merchants to create a world-class credit report. When you complete the following process, it is going to revolutionize your financial life. If you have had a cash flow problem, for the first time ever, the light will go off and you'll say, "Wow!" Channeling your spending power will put you in control of your financial life. This is not a book about money, but I strongly believe that designing your credit report will form a strong foundation to your financial fortress. Designing your credit report involves controlling your credit activities in the following areas:

1. Revolving account
    a. Visa card
    b. MasterCard
    c. Diners card
    d. Department store
    e. Gas card

2. Nonrevolving or installment
    a. Personal loan
    b. Car loan
    c. Boat loan
    d. Mortgage loan
    e. Equity loan
    f. School loan
    g. Electronic loan
    h. Appliance loan
    i. Furniture store
    j. Jewelry store

Attacking Your Negative Cash Flow

An interest payment is an impediment on the road to financial success. The less you pay in interest, the more cash flow you have for other expenses. The system you have in your hands will help you break the negative cash flow cycle in your life. Let's review this unending cycle that devours your hard-earned money.

- When you have low cash flow, you make late payments.

- When you make late payments, you have a low credit score.

- When you have a low credit score, you pay more in interest.

- When you pay more in interest, you have low cash flow and are back at square one. This is the perpetual cycle of negative cash flow.

What if you monitor your credit report successfully and see your credit score accelerate to the highest level, would your cash flow not improve tremendously? Absolutely! And…

- When you have more cash flow, you make payments on time.

- When you make payments on time, you have a high credit score.

- When you have a high credit score, you pay little or no interest.

- When you pay little or no interest, you have more cash flow and are back at the beginning. This is the perpetual cycle of positive cash flow.

If you act today and repair your credit, there is no doubt your credit score will go up. And when your credit score goes up, everybody wants to sell you something. Believe me, news will get out that you're a good customer, and your name will be included in the list of buying elite. Don't forget merchants pay big money to credit bureaus get this list. Guess what? You're now one of the buying elite. Because you repaired your own credit, and know how to choose quality and friendly merchants—you're now in control of everything you buy, and, ultimately, in control of your credit report.

When you design and control your credit report with quality merchants, the world would take notice. These quality merchants will charge little or no interest. In fact, they give their customers interest-free purchases for as long as they want it. You are now one of the elite who doesn't pay interest on merchandise he buys, and that translates into more cash in your pocket. This is what good cash flow is all about—keeping more of your money.

Chapter 14

Reasons for a Low Credit Score

You Don't Know the Value of a Score

Let's face it, if you had known you would be losing thousands of dollars each year because of some stupid number assigned by someone on information supplied by some businesses, you would have been very careful about making sure your payments were recorded on your credit report correctly. Here you are, working so hard and making an honest effort to pay your bills, but for some reason, when your payments didn't make it to the merchant on time either by wrong delivery or by business error, you are reported to the credit bureau, and your dirty laundry is shown to the prospective merchants.

Would it make any difference if the businesses had written you to tell you that in 30 days, they would be reporting your late payment to the credit bureau? You bet, it would! No, businesses do not have to write customers about reporting them to the credit bureaus or about lowering their credit score. Sometimes, consumers don't even know if a particular transaction is a reportable or nonreportable transaction to the credit bureau.

I've met a lot of people who have not even heard about credit scores much less credit bureaus. So, when they see a low credit score, which determines what percentage interest they deserve—20%, they don't even ask why. They are very happy their credit application is approved in the first place. Some people even think credit bureaus are nonprofit organizations appointed by the government to keep scores on what they buy, and whatever they say is the law. Therefore, they are pleased with any score as long as their credit request is granted—any interest rate is celebrated.

Many people are spending thousands of dollars each year on purchases that do not count on their credit score, by paying cash or by dealing with merchants that do not report to the credit bureau. Instead of writing a $1,000 check to a furniture company, you could have deposited that cash into separate checking account. And then buy the furniture on credit and pay it off with the $1,000 in the bank, say $100 a month for 10 months as discussed previously. When you repeat this process on every high-dollar item you buy, not only will your credit score be very high, but your financial mentality will be second to none. Now that you know the value of a good credit score, you should use the following steps to improve it:

1.   Review your credit report every year.
2.   Buy anything only as a way to increase your credit score.
3.   Buy only from businesses that report to the credit bureaus.
4.   Buy only from quality businesses that would ignore a few mistakes—quality merchants will waive reporting late payments.
5.   Make sure every mistake on your credit report is corrected.
6.   Pay your bills on time to avoid late fees.
7.   Live within your means by buying only the things you need, not the things you want.
8.   Don't buy on credit unless you have deposited the cash into a separate checking account.
9.   Pay off your credit card each month.
10.   Put a cap on how much you can put on the credit card each month.
11.   Stay away from places that force you to use your credit card recklessly.

You Don't Know Merchants' Policies

If consumers have never heard about a credit score or credit bureaus, most likely, they have never heard about merchants reporting their payment activities to the credit bureaus. Some merchants report to all three major credit bureaus, others report to one or two. The principles discussed below are applicable to a variety of merchants. Before you do business with any merchant, you must know their reporting policies. Let us review some credit reporting policies of the following businesses, which are applicable to other businesses:

•   Credit card companies

•   Auto finance companies

Credit card companies. They report directly to the credit bureau. Most credit card companies will tell you when you are late and will give you time to take care of it. Good credit card companies are willing to overlook your first late payment and not report it. Make sure you have a letter that says your account was not reported to the credit bureau. If a credit card company quickly reports you to the credit bureau, immediately talk to a manager or a supervisor and try to get a one-time courtesy forgiveness on your late payment. Most "loan sharks" are hard to deal with, and should be avoided at all costs. Credit card companies will do the following:

- Review your credit
- May demand deposit for a secured credit if you have a low score
- May do a charge-off on your account
- May use an in-house or outside collection agency
- May sell account to a collection agency
- Report directly your monthly activities to the bureau
- Not have any asset to repossess
- May or may not take you to court
- May purge accounts three to five years old
- May negotiate a deal for scheduled payment.

Auto finance companies. Anytime you walk into a Ford dealership to buy or lease a car, Ford Credit has the right of first refusal. That is, Ford will first run a credit check on you to determine if you're a good credit risk. If Ford refuses you, something is wrong. Most likely, your credit is below their threshold. Then, the dealership will shop around and try to finance you through a credit union or a finance company. These finance companies talk about only one thing—interest! They eat and breathe interest. Most of them are hard to deal with, especially when it comes to late payments. In fact, some finance companies are worse than collection agencies. Finance companies employ their new recruits from collection agencies. You must send in your payment ahead of the due date.

Ask to speak to the manager or the supervisor of the finance companies, but understand that most of the time, managers and supervisors will tell you exactly what the sales person has already told you. They are not really helpful when it comes to waiving your first-time late payment. They are ruthless and, therefore, you should do everything to avoid the finance companies. At all costs, try to get your financing from Ford Credit, GMAC, a credit division of a car company, a bank, or a credit union. Finance companies will do the following:

- Review your credit
- Ask for little or no down payment
- May not do a charge-off on your account
- May use an in-house or outside collection agency
- May sell account to a collection agency
- Report directly your monthly activities to the bureau
- Repossess your car, sell it, and come after the difference
- Take you to court if the difference is huge
- May purge accounts three to five years old
- Some will not negotiate, they want full payment

When it comes to correcting your credit report, the merchants are your formidable allies and are willing to help you at all times. Most books on credit repair are geared toward the credit bureaus. They place much emphasis on the credit reporting agencies and how to dispute and beg them to change your credit score. You are playing right into the hands of the credit bureaus by emphasizing their importance the way most books do.

This book is taking a proactive approach by emphasizing the importance of merchants and collection agencies rather than the credit bureaus. Let me repeat—the credit bureaus are just messengers, and their job is to collect information—right or wrong. Your job is to find out what information they have on you that is wrong and ask them to correct it—with the law on your side. How can you spend less time with the person who created the information and more with the person who keeps the information? The reverse should be the case—spending more time with merchants and less time with the messengers who keep the information.

Since we know the importance of merchants, we should find out the proper ways to work with them. The best way to work with a merchant is first to find the best merchant to do business with. What if you were to choose between good and bad teachers, would you not choose a good teacher who cares to teach and who will not fail you just because you make few mistakes?

Well, in the credit-reporting world, you have a choice. You can choose which merchants you want to deal with. Before you initiate a business transaction with any merchant, think about your credit report and credit score. You can choose what names you want the world to see on your report. The kind of merchants you have on your report can tell a prospective lender everything about you. For example, you don't have to tell anyone about your taste and lifestyle when you have names such as Nieman Marcus, Macy's, Ethan Allen, Jaguar, and Mercedes on your credit report. Therefore, your job is to design your credit report to present yourself as a quality consumer. You already know that prospective merchants treat quality customers exceptionally better than the general public.

You Don't Know Credit Bureaus' Policies

The credit reporting agencies or credit bureaus have been accused of all kinds of things, mostly because the public does not understand their duties and obligations. The credit bureaus are merely messengers when you understand the laws governing their activities. I have seen materials in which authors advised readers to argue or negotiate with credit bureaus. You do not argue or negotiate with credit bureaus, you tell them what to do, according to the law—which is the only thing they respect.

In fairness, I think the credit reporting agencies are doing a good job in collecting credit information. However, it is a different story when it comes to correcting their mistakes. Most of the problems come from the fact that the general public does not know the credit bureaus' activities, which the law has granted them to know. Consumers are very upset with credit bureaus when they see their credit score for the first time, especially if it is very low. They do not understand that the business of compiling credit information on adults in this country is an awesome task. Once you initiate the first credit transaction, and a file is opened on you, more transactions will automatically trigger an unending flow of credit information into your credit file. The credit bureaus are not in the business of immediately verifying the accuracy of the information that is pouring in on your behalf. Understand that it is impossible to scrutinize every transaction on every person before it is entered into the computer.

The credit bureaus assume all data is correct or "innocent until proven guilty." They will wait to see if John Doe, for example, actually exists. If John Doe knows the value of his credit score, he will not be so gullible or foolish as to accept a preliminary score of 650 when he deserves 845. Did you get that? The credit bureaus know that John Doe does not deserve the score of 650 but only if he can come forth and tell them how to change it to a higher number. Don't plead or beg them—it is your credit report.

You need to know that your credit score, before you start cleaning it up, is just a preliminary number and is sometimes called the Prelim Score. It is your job, not the credit bureaus' job, to verify every entry on your credit report. When you have cleaned up your credit report, you will be given a score of 845 or above. It is at this point that the preliminary score becomes the real score. When you see a score that you don't like, don't get upset with the messenger but with the message—sent by merchants and collection agencies.

Once you understand this basic principle, you'll never get angry or upset with the credit bureau's preliminary score. They are in the business of gathering, storing, and disseminating credit information. Credit bureaus are not in the business of investigating whether you made your payment on time or not; it is your responsibility to investigate your payment and your credit score.

When you receive your credit report, it will have different sections. Remember that in the credit reporting business the only thing that doesn't change is you. The credit reporting format changes all the time. Addresses, phone numbers, everything changes. You will bear witness to this truth when you start cleaning up your credit report—guaranteed!

Besides the merchants, credit bureaus are your greatest allies. You should know how to work with them, too. The secret to working with credit bureaus is knowing your rights. Any time you write or talk to the credit bureaus, you should think "legal" and "your right." However, you should minimize legal words in your letters and phone calls. They will work with you when they discover you know your rights without screaming your rights at them.

How can they tell if you know your rights? Your first letter will tell them you know your rights or know what you are doing. Your letters should be professional and to the point. Professionalism does not mean the way you sound in your letter, rather the steps you take in approaching the credit bureaus. For example, you could write your letter by hand to the credit bureaus and it could still be very professional because it would contain the essential elements that would get you instant results.

With your first letter, the credit bureaus could tell if you don't know the credit laws and processes. Knowledge of your rights and the laws is a requirement to effectively deal with merchants, collection agencies, and credit bureaus. You must read and understand section seven—dealing with government agencies. That section is one of the most important parts of the entire book, because it contains your basic rights as a consumer. You must understand that credit laws change all the time, and on your first free consultation with an attorney, your task is to know how these laws have changed. Your attorney will be glad to answer your questions, because of the way you communicate with him or her. Professionals like to deal with knowledgeable clients. In other words, clients who have done some research, and because of this book, you are one of them—guaranteed!

Chapter 15

Who Reports the Most Negative Entries?

Who Reports the Most Negative Entries

I have saved the best for last! This is one of the most important topics in the entire book. For one reason or the other, there are certain businesses that are not allowed to report your transaction activities to the credit bureau. One of the reasons is that these activities are not debt related. In other words, you did not go to these companies and borrow money or merchandise from them with promise to pay. Unlike credit card companies or department store companies, these activities are regarded as necessities; therefore, you are allowed to pay as you receive services. Understanding how to deal with these companies is going to save you thousands of dollars—not to mention peace of mind—guaranteed!

These companies do not report your good and bad credit activities to the credit bureau, but they use your credit score to determine the fees they charge you. Because everyone has to deal with the utility companies—one way or the other, 90% of your credit problems will come from these companies. If you master the strategies on how to deal with them, your credit score will be in the top percentile. The following businesses and credit activities are hard to deal with most on your credit report:

Utility companies
1.   Cell phone companies
2.   Telephone companies
3.   Gas and electric companies

Medical industries
1.   Hospitals
2.   Doctors and laboratories

Government-related debt
1.   Taxes and bankruptcy
2.   School loans

Why They Report the Most Negative Entries

The reason these businesses are quick to report your bad credit history to the credit bureau—is money—short and simple! The bottom line is money—very easy money! The earlier they can send your name to the credit bureau, the earlier other companies in the same business can charge you the highest interest rates, the highest down payment, the highest connection fees, etc.—the highest of everything—in the name of security or protection from business risk. Businesses that check your credit are doing so just for this reason.

These businesses operate as follows:

Utility companies

Utility companies include cellular phone companies, telephone companies and gas and electric companies. I have intentionally separated the cellular phone companies from the telephone companies because of the aggressiveness of the cellular phone companies. Telephone companies own the cables that run through your home and business, but cellular phone companies do not own the cables; they sell you minutes and their cellular phones. Utility companies do not report your monthly payments to the credit bureau, because it is just a bill and not a debt. However, as soon as you are 30 days late, they cut your off services and report you to the credit bureau.

Customer services. The utility companies have the worst customer service of any company I have ever seen. They do not care about their customers. The first thing you want to note when setting up your service is how long it takes you to talk to a live person. How many telephone prompts do you hear and how many minutes do you have to wait before you talk to an individual? If service during set up is not friendly or smooth, do not deal with that company. The pain of correcting errors on your bill is 10 times the pain of setting up your services. Watch out for red flags when you find it difficult to set up the services you want for the price you want.

Billing. Watch out for bait and switch, in which the company will agree to a lower rate but when you get your bill, it is padded with services and fees they want to gouge from you. Utility companies operate on an average bill; this is the amount of money they must gouge from every customer. Their attitude is you pay what we bill you or else we cut your services off and ruin your credit report. Another kind of bait and switch is the limited time promotion. Never buy service that has conditions like, "five cents per minute for three months, or $12.99 per month for six months and for credit cards, zero percent interest free for six months." These companies will not tell you what they will do to you after the three or six months. They will charge you the maximum amount they didn't want you to know about in the first place. Don't forget their motive—if you don't pay the bill, they will cut off your service and report you to the credit bureaus. This is their only motive.

End of contract. You must know the duration of your contract and if there are early termination fees and a number of days to return your phone without any termination fees. If you decide to keep your services, pay your bill on time. Late fees are very costly. If you're not able to make your payments, and want to keep the service, cut off all extra services and keep only the basic plan. If you are unable to pay even the basic bill and want to cut off the services, keep your last bill. Guard the last bill as you guard your birth certificate. Whatever you do, try and pay the last bill unless there is an error on the bill. The following are the steps the cellular phone companies will take against you when you did not pay your bill:

a.   They will cut off your services and send you the last bill.
b.   They will send your account to the cellular phone collection department.
c.   After 30 days, you will start getting annoying calls from the cellular phone collection department.
d.   After 30 days, the cellular phone collection department will report your account to the credit bureau as delinquent.
e.   The name of the cellular phone collection department will be listed on your credit report. It will have a different name from the name of the cellular phone company and the amount reported to the credit bureau might be different from the amount on the last bill.
f.   After 30 to 120 days, the cellular phone collection department will continue to harass you to force you to pay.
g.   After 120 days, the cellular phone collection department will sell your account to an outside collection agency for 50 cents on a dollar or

assign the account to an outside collection agency on a 50/50 commission basis.

Medical industry

The medical industry includes hospitals, doctors' offices, and laboratories. The medical industry is not as aggressive and harassing as utility companies. They do not report you to the credit bureau until you're unable to pay your bill 30 days after you received it.

Customer services. In the past, you provided your insurance card and Social Security number to the in-take staff at the hospital, doctor's office or laboratory before you saw the doctor, but with the change in the law, you now only provide your insurance card. You must never give your Social Security card or number to anybody. If you're older than 18, you must sign your own paper work. Do not sign the financial responsibility form for anyone else unless they are a minor. If the bill is not paid, you will limit ruining only one person's credit report instead of everybody's in the family who signs the papers. Even if you have 10 people under your coverage, do not sign any paper with the hospital except in a case of a major operation in which the doctor will need a family member to sign for the medical services, not the financial responsibility. Write, "Not financially responsible" beside your signature.

Billing. Medical industry billing practices are the worst of any industry. Some mistakes are mere typing errors and others are fraudulent attempts to pad your medical bill with extra charges or services you did not receive. If you have chronic medical illness, it is advisable to have medical insurance; that way you can limit the amount of expenses to your co-payments or deductible. After you enroll with an insurance company, you will be given a card that has your co-payment written on the back. The co-payment or deductible is the amount you will pay to the doctor or pharmacy. You will also be assigned to a primary care physician (PCP). Your PCP is responsible for minor illnesses, such as headaches, colds, and the flu. If your case needs a specialist, he or she will refer you to a specialist according to the insurance company direction.

When you see your PCP, you will provide your insurance card for verification. After you've seen the doctor, you make your co-payment or deductible and the case is closed. Because you've paid your premium and your co-payment or deductible, the doctor should charge the remaining balance to the insurance company on what has been previously agreed upon.

If your PCP thinks the case should be referred to a specialist, you will be sent to one in the field of your illness. The specialist will call the insurance company to get authorization. The authorization will preapprove what it will take to get you well. When you see the specialist, you will make your co-payment and the specialist will bill the balance to the insurance company according to the pre-approval agreement.

This is where mistakes are made. You must read this section very carefully. When your PCP, who has an agreement with the insurance company on what it will take to get you well, bills more than that amount, it will be sent to the insurance company, who pays only what was agreed upon. If the PCP billed what was not agreed upon, and the insurance company does not pay the full amount on the bill, the PCP will send the unpaid portion to you for payment. At this point, you should call the PCP ask why you're being billed. If the insurance company paid any portion of the bill, the rest is written off. If the insurance company did not pay any portion, work with the insurance company to pay what was agreed upon and the rest will be written off. The same goes with the specialist. After you've paid your premium and your co-payment, you should not pay a penny more to the hospital, doctor, or laboratory. Most people do not know this, and when they get the bill, they toss it in a file—this is a big mistake. After 30 days the account is reported to the credit bureau. The following are the steps the medical industry will take after you do not pay your bill:

a.   They will send your bill to the insurance company to pay.
b.   If the insurance company does not pay off the bill, the medical entity will send you a bill for the remaining balance.
c.   After 30 days, you may get a call from the collection department of the medical entity.
d.   After 30 days, your account is sold or assigned to a collection agency that reports the account to the credit bureau immediately.
e.   The name of the collection agency is listed on your credit report.

f.   After one year or so, the first collection agency will sell the account or assign it to another collection agency.

g.   The second collection agency will report the same account to the credit bureau with a different account number and possibly with a different amount to confuse you.

Government-related debt

The four major government-related debts are bankruptcies, tax liens, school loan, and child support. These are the hardest negative entries to remove from your credit report. The good news is that there are strategies you can use to remove these entries from your credit report.

How they get into your report. For bankruptcies, tax liens, and child support, credit bureaus use contractor or freelance agents to scout the court records to update the credit bureaus' database everyday. Remember, the more the credit bureau updates your file, the more it sells the correct information to your "enemies" who may be looking for you. So, every time you apply for credit, they will update your file and immediately call your "enemies" to sell them information on you. Sometimes, these companies pay huge monthly fees so that the credit bureau will contact them anytime the bureau has important information on you, such as better job.

Sallie Mae is the major government contractor on school loans. It will never come off your credit report until it is paid in full, and sometimes, they will stop and collect your tax refunds for the loan.

Government-related debt enters your credit report as follows:

a.   For bankruptcies, tax liens, and child support, after the case has gone through the legal system, your case is shown in court records for the amount of bankruptcy, tax lien, or child support.

b.   For bankruptcies, all your debt is wiped off with only the bankruptcy amount showing.

c.   The credit bureaus will use freelance agents or their own staff to update their records for bankruptcies, tax liens, and child support.

d.   For bankruptcies, the credit bureaus will delete all your previous debts and will enter only one negative entry—the bankruptcy and its amount.

e.   For school loans, when you default on your payment to Sallie Mae, it will report your late payment to the credit bureau.

f.   If you are three to six months late, it may sell your account back to the government who guaranteed the loan. The government will sell the account to a collection agency, which will report the same account to the credit bureau under its name and maybe with a different amount.

How to Deal with These Entities

In this section, we are going to look at the strategies you would use to prevent these companies from gouging your hard-earned money. Any time you wonder why these companies are hounding you, think about your credit report. The earlier they can get your bill to the credit bureau, the earlier the rest of the companies in that industry and everybody else will be picking your pocket. If you learn how to handle these entities before they send you to the credit bureau, your credit life will never be the same—guaranteed!

Utility companies

The best way to prevent the utility companies from picking your pocket is as follows:

a.   Know the exact services you're getting.
b.   Write the exact services you need.
c.   Write the exact amount you will see on your bill each month and confirm this with the representative who is setting up your services.
d.   Write down how much it will cost if you go over your minutes, if any.
e.   Write the date you can return the cellular phone without any charges, if any.

f.   Write the date the contract will expire, if any.
g.   Write down how much it will cost for early cancellation of the contract.
h.   Write down what date you will receive the sign-up package.
i.   Write down any other information that will help you to match the amount and services during the set up with the amount and services on the bill you will receive at the end of the month.
j.   Make sure that when you receive your sign-up package, the services and prices match what the customer service personnel quoted.
k.   If they are not the same, call and demand correction; otherwise, return the phone and cancel the contract (with registered mail) because your problems are just beginning.
l.   Return the phone before the date you can do so without any charges.
m.   If you decide to keep your service, make sure the charges quoted match the charges on the actual bill.
n.   If possible, get unlimited minutes; that way you know your bill is fixed each month.
o.   Anytime you call the utility company, write down the date, time (do this while you're waiting for someone to pick up the phone), the representative and what he or she said.
p.   Let the representative know you're writing down their statement by making them repeat their name and spell it at the end of the conversation.
q.   Pay your last bill immediately when you and the company come to an agreement.

Medical industry

The best strategies to apply with the medical industry are as follows:

a.   It is important to get medical insurance, especially if you have a chronic illness.
b.   Look for an insurance company that has "a mutual company" by its name. This is applicable with financial and insurance industries. Their prices and services are much better than others. This will save you a lot of money.

c.   Pay your co-payment. Most $5-$20 negative entries on credit reports I have seen are unpaid co-payments. These small amounts could be costing you 50 -100 points on your credit score.

d.   When you receive a bill from a hospital, doctor, or laboratory, if the insurance company does not pay any money at all, you are either suspended for nonpayment of premium or the insurance company does not verify your paperwork correctly as a customer. Tell the insurance company to call the doctor to verify that you are his patient.

e.   If the insurance company pays only some, that is the amount they approved and agreed upon with the doctor to treat you. You have to ask the doctor to write off the balance. You should not pay a dime if the doctor overbilled the insurance company and now wants to come after you for the balance. They will write it off if you say so. This will save you a lot of money.

f.   You want the doctor or hospital to send you a zero balance bill. If not, call your insurance company; they will make the doctor write it off, because they approved what it will take to cure you.

g.   Keep the bill in a safe place until you receive the zero balance; otherwise, your account may be sold at a later date with the delinquent amount changed to confuse you.

h.   If any member of your household is older than 18, they should sign their own authorization for treatment. Do not sign authorization for treatment unless the medical treatment is for a minor.

i.   Do not tell the in-take staff your Social Security number or give the in-take staff the actual Social Security card.

Government-related debt

The best strategies to use in dealing with government related debt are as follows:

a.   For school loans, keep records of the actual amount and date of the debt.

b.   Quickly agree upon installment payments you can afford.

c.   If you agree to an installment payment, you will get Sallie Mae to report the loan as "paying as agreed" or the collection agency to delete its name and the negative entry from your credit report.

d.   For tax liens, keep records of the actual amount and date of the debt.

e.   Before the IRS files the tax lien, negotiate with the agency on "offer for compromise," that is agreeing on how much you can give the IRS to settle the debt.

f.   If you do not have enough money to pay the taxes, that is if the IRS calculates your living expenses and nothing is left, the IRS may release the debt and the tax lien.

g.   For child support, you must agree to a monthly payment so the case is not filed in the first place.

h.   For bankruptcy, you must know the amount of bankruptcy.

i.   Remember, that merchants welcome people that have filed for bankruptcy because they know you cannot file another bankruptcy and, therefore, must pay your bill.

j.   The best strategy is to flood your credit report with new positive entries. Because all your negative entries are deleted and you have only one negative entry, which is the bankruptcy, your best approach is to use the secured personal loan strategy discussed in this book.

k.   If you flood your credit report with the new entry strategies in this book, in less time than you think, your credit score will be in the highest bracket.

l.   For the bankruptcy entry itself, the best action is to wait for it to expire.

I know you will never forget that there are only two steps to increasing your credit score—cleaning your credit report and adding new credit entries. If you apply the principles suggested in this book, your credit score will never be the same.

Appendix

Credit Bureau Information:

Equifax
P.O. Box 740241
Atlanta, GA 30374

1-800-685-111

Experian
701 Experian Pkwy
Allen, TX 75013

P.O. Box 2104
Allen, TX 75013

1-888-EXPERIAN

TransUnion
P.O. Box 2000
Chester, PA 19022

1-800-888-4213

Credit Report Sources:

Annual Credit Report Services
P.O. Box 105283
Atlanta, GA 30348

1-877-322-8228

VantageScore Solutions
www.vantagescore.com

Credit-Related Laws

Federal Trade Commission

1. Visit www.ftc.gov.
2. Click For Consumers on the left-hand side
3. Click Credit on the left-hand side
4. Click Rules & Acts at the top of the page
5. Look for the following acts:
   a. Credit Repair Organization Act
   b. Equal Credit Opportunity Act
   c. Fair Credit Billing Act
   d. Fair Credit Reporting Act—Home Page
   e. Fair Debt Collection Practices Act—Home Page

6. Click **Credit Repair Organization Act**
   Browse through the act.

7. Click **Equal Credit Opportunity Act**
   Browse through the act.

8. Click **Fair Credit Billing Act**
   Browse through the act.

9. Click **Fair Credit Reporting Act**—Home Page
   Click **Fair Credit Reporting Act** on the left-had side
   You may have to wait. Browse through the act.
   Click the Back arrow button at the top of the monitor
   Click the **Fair and Accurate Credit Transaction Act** on the right-hand side
   Browse through the act.
   Click the Back arrow button at the top of the monitor.

10. Click **Fair Debt Collection Practices Act**—Home Page
    Click **Fair Debt Collection Practices Act** on the left-hand side
    Browse through the act.
    Click the Back arrow button at the top of the monitor.

SOW Publishing

Visit our Web site and see other published books or books in the process of being published. If you want a product catalog, price list, or other information, e-mail sales@sowpublishing.com. You can also purchase some of our books from Barnes & Noble Booksellers, www.amazon.com, or anywhere books are sold. For bulk discount purchase e-mail publisher@sowpublishing.com

Our products include the following:

1.	Using Quicken with High Speed

2.	Using Quicken with High Speed Workbook

3.	Using QuickBooks with High Speed

4.	Using QuickBooks with High Speed Workbook

5.	How to Increase Your Credit Score—Kit

6.	How to Increase Your Credit Score—Book

7.	How to Repair Your Credit Score—Book

8.	Using Excel with High Speed—Book

9.	Using Word with High Speed—Book

10.	Creating Wealth with Stocks and Options—Book

Visit www.sowpublishing.com

Printed in the United States
69954LV00004B/53-56

9 780977 069330